Zaner-Bloser
Handwriting
A Way to Self-Expression

W9-COY-470

Senior Authors

Clinton S. Hackney, Ed.D.
Language Arts Consultant

Virginia H. Lucas, Ph.D.
Professor of Education
Wittenberg University

Grade 2c

Contributing Authors

Janet T. Bercik, Ed.D.
Coordinator of Clinical Experiences
Northeastern Illinois University

Stephen E. Rogalski, B.S.
Fourth Grade Teacher
New Martinsville (W.V.) School

Wilma J. Farmer, Ed.D.
Director of Elementary Education
Camden (N.J.) City School District

James A. Wilhide, Ed.D.
Former Language Arts Consultant
South Carolina State Department of Education

Gloria C. Rivera, M.A.
Former Elementary Supervisor
Zapata County (Texas) I.S.D.

Consultants

Marsha Brown, Blue Valley (Kans.) Unified School District 229
Sondra Shepherd, Benton Harbor (Mich.) Area School District
Marsha Urban, Omaha City School District 1

Valerie A. Elinski, Diocese of Buffalo (N.Y.)
Laura L. Stokes, Princeville (Ill.) Community School District

Credits

Literature: "Look in a Book" by Ivy O. Eastwick. Copyright © 1978 by Highlights for Children, Inc. "Signposts" *Houghton Mifflin Reading,* copyright © 1971. Used with permission of Houghton Mifflin Company. P. 20 (Untitled): from *Run, Zebra, Run* by Tony Chen. Copyright © 1972 by Tony Chen. Reprinted by permission of Lothrop, Lee & Shepard Books, a division of William Morrow & Co. "A New Friend" by Marjorie Allen Anderson from *Away We Go! 100 Poems for the Very Young.* Compiled by Catherine Schaefer McEwen. Copyright © 1956 Catherine Schaefer McEwen. Reprinted by permission of HarperCollins Publishers. "Where People Live" by Lois Lenski from *The Life I Live, Collected Poems,* Henry Z. Walch, Inc., New York, copyright © 1965. "Just Me" by Margaret Hillert. Used by permission of Margaret Hillert who controls all rights. "Don't Ever Cross a Crocodile" from *Don't Ever Cross a Crocodile* by Kaye Starbird, J. B. Lippencott Co., copyright © 1963. By permission of the author. "Butterfly Wings" from *In the Woods, In the Meadow, In the Sky.* New York: Scribner's, 1965. By permission of the author. "The Elephant's Trunk" by Irma V. Sanderson. Copyright © 1981. Used by permission of Highlights for Children, Inc. "At the Library" from *Rhymes About Us* by Marchette Chute. Copyright © 1974 by E. P. Dutton, Inc. Reprinted by permission of Mary Chute Smith. "Tell Me A

Story" by Alice Low from *People & Places* by Margaret Early. Copyright © 1979 by Harcourt Brace Jovanovich, Inc., reprinted by permission of the publisher. "Thomas F. Turtle" by Kathryn Gelander. Copyright © 1973. Used by permission of Highlights for Children, Inc.

Photos: p. 9: James P. Rowan/TSW-Click/Chicago; p. 10: Walter Wright/H. Armstrong Roberts; p. 14: MacDonald Photography/Third Coast Stock Source; p. 15: Robert Frerck/TSW-Click/Chicago; p. 19: Index Stock; pp. 20-21: Gerry Ellis/Ellis Wildlife. Joe McDonald, Nancy Adams/Tom Stack & Associates; pp. 28-29: Bob McKeever/Tom Stack & Associates. Comstock. J. Spratt, J. Nettis/H. Armstrong Roberts. Lisa Valder/TSW-Click/Chicago; p. 31: Peter Miller/The Image Bank; p. 34: J. Myers/H. Armstrong Roberts; pp. 40-41: Froebisch/Zefa/H. Armstrong Roberts; p. 44: Devaney Stock Photos. AP/Wide World; p. 51: Robin Smith/TSW-Click/Chicago; pp. 60-61: Devaney Stock Photos; p. 67: Peter Miller/The Image Bank; p. 72: D. Seman/Marilyn Gartman Agency; p. 73: Zefa/H. Armstrong Roberts; p. 76: Laurence Hughes/The Image Bank. Robert Daemmrich/TSW-Click/Chicago; p. 79: Larry Brock/Tom Stack & Associates; p. 81: Carol Lee/TSW-Click/Chicago; p. 84: Peter Miller/The Image Bank;

p. 85: Robin Forbes/The Image Bank; p. 86: Martin Rogers/TSW-Click/Chicago; p. 92: Superstock; p. 106: Gary Brettnacher/TSW-Click/Chicago; p. 109: K. Strand/H. Armstrong Roberts; p. 112: Stephen Marks/The Image Bank; p. 114: Stuart Cohen/Comstock; p. 116: Ted Kawalerski/The Image Bank; p. 118: G & J Images/The Image Bank; p. 120: Kuhn, Inc./The Image Bank; p. 121: L. Burton/H. Armstrong Roberts; p. 123: Alastair Black/TSW-Click/Chicago; pp. 126-127: H. Armstrong Roberts. Camerique/H. Armstrong Roberts. Brian Seed/TSW-Click/Chicago. Jay Freis, Alan Becker, Peter Miller, Flip Chalfant, Don Klumpp/The Image Bank; p. 135: Nancy Brown/The Image Bank; p. 136: Christopher Crowley/Tom Stack & Associates.

Art: Liz Allen: pp. 22, 36, 58 (right), 63-65, 69, 78-79, 97, 102, 105, 133, 139; Gwen Connelly: pp. 2-3, 12-13, 16-17, 24-25, 42-43, 45-47, 54-55, 68, 77, 108, 125, 128-129, 132, 141; Lulu Delacre: p. 124; Dennis Hockerman: pp. 56-57, 71, 75, 83, 110-111, 130-131, 137, 140; Loretta Lustig: pp. 8, 18, 65; James Needham: pp. 32-33, 53, 91; Stella Ormai: pp. 11, 37-39, 48-49, 64, 99, 101, 107, 117, 138-139; Jeff Severn: pp. 80, 96, 103, 115; Sally Springer: pp. 6-7, 23, 26-27, 30, 35, 50, 52, 58 (left), 59, 62, 70, 82, 87-89, 93, 104, 113, 134.

Design and production by The Quarasan Group, Inc.
Cover Photo: Aaron Haupt

ISBN 0-88085-169-4

94 95 96 97 DP 8 7 6 5 4

Copyright © 1993 Zaner-Bloser, Inc.

Table of Contents

MANUSCRIPT

CURSIVE

LOWERCASE LETTERS

UPPERCASE LETTERS

Pretest

Look in a Book

Look in a book
and you will see
words and magic
and mystery.

Look in a book
and you will find
sense and nonsense
of every kind.

Look in a book
and you will know
all the things that
can help you grow.

Ivy O. Eastwick

Write the first verse of the poem. Use your best handwriting.

Keys to Legibility Score Box		
Check:	Satisfactory	Needs to Improve
size	☐	☐
shape	☐	☐
slant	☐	☐
spacing	☐	☐
smoothness	☐	☐

3

Manuscript Refinement

Signposts

Signposts . . . signposts . . .
What do they say?
"School Ahead"
Or "Children at Play",
"Don't Feed the Animals",
"Slow", "For Sale",
"Keep off the Grass",
"Don't Lean On the Rail".
Signposts . . . signposts . . .
Have SO much to say,
And each is important
In its very own way.

Vivian Gouled

Basic Strokes

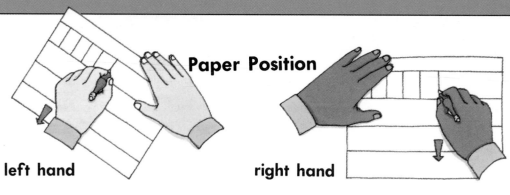

Paper Position

left hand   right hand

Vertical lines

Pull down straight

Push up straight

fish _____ hill _____ little _____

Horizontal lines

Slide right

Slide left

I_ E_ F_ D_ B_ P_ R_

Helen _____ Robert _____

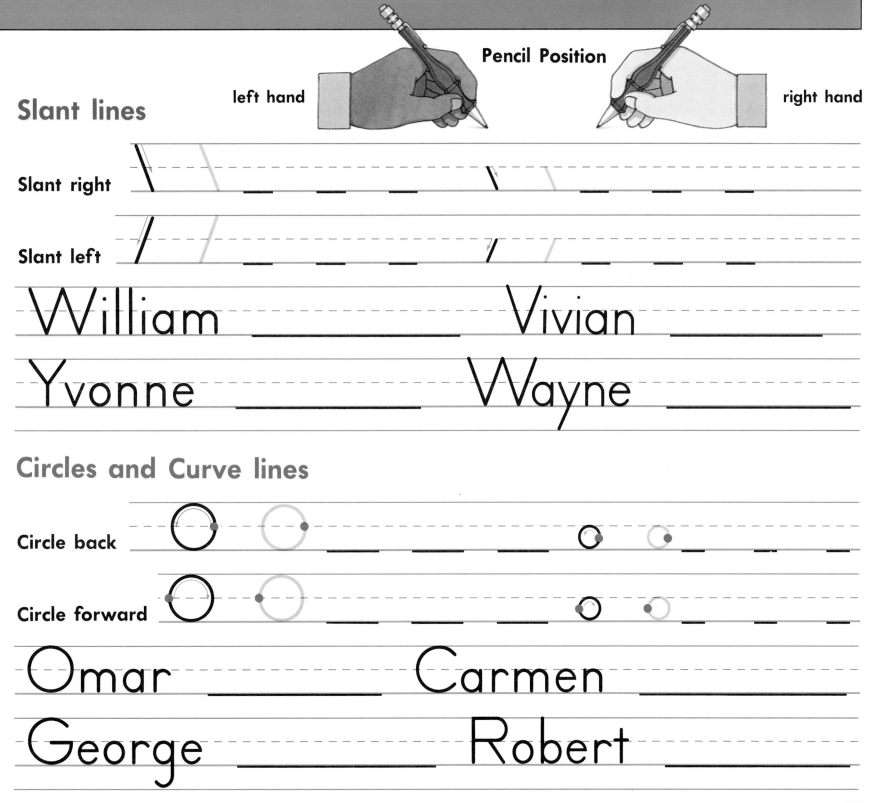

Slant lines

Pencil Position

left hand   right hand

Slant right

Slant left

William _____   Vivian _____

Yvonne _____   Wayne _____

Circles and Curve lines

Circle back

Circle forward

Omar _____   Carmen _____

George _____   Robert _____

Trace and write.

lesson

library

L

L

Linda

Lincoln

l L

Write an advertisement
for a book in your library.

Lincoln Library

8

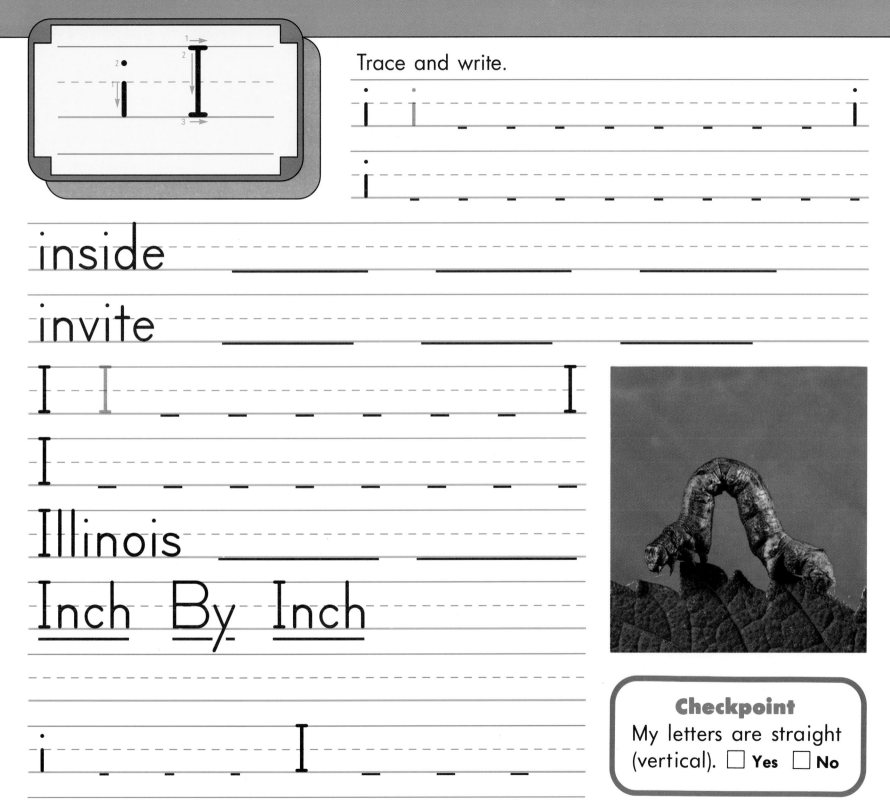

Trace and write.

i i · · · · · · · · · · i

i · · · · · · · · · · ·

inside

invite

I I · · · · · · · · · I

I · · · · · · · · · ·

Illinois

Inch By Inch

i · · · · · I · · · ·

Checkpoint

My letters are straight (vertical). ☐ **Yes** ☐ **No**

9

t T

Trace and write.

t t t   t

t

travel

train

T T   T

T

Texas

Ted slept on the train.

t   T

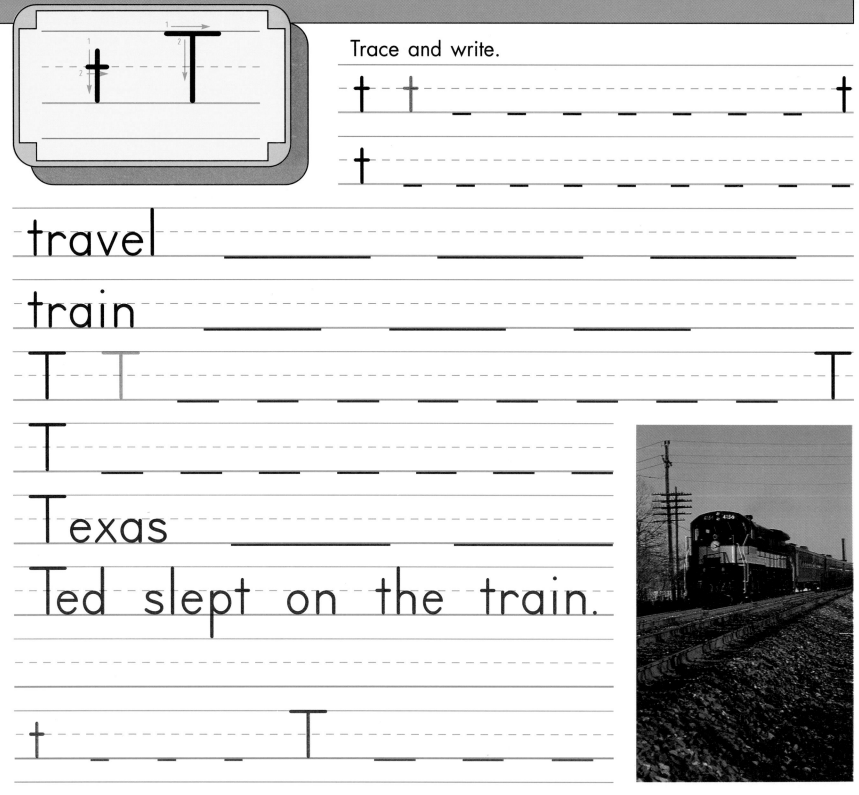

Numerals

1. Write the license numbers for the three cars.

_____ _____ _____

2. How far is it to Austin? _____

3. What exit is next? _____

4. How far is it to Arlington? _____

5. What is the number of the interstate? _____

Our Town

I like to walk to town each day
And visit shops along the way.
Sometimes I buy a toy or book
And other times I stop and look.

Lou's Light Shop

Unknown

Toy Store

Ike's Inn

Library

Write the poem.

1. Write the name of the place where you find books.

2. Write the name of the store where you might buy a lamp.

3. Write the name of the store where you might buy a teddy bear.

4. Write the name of the place where people sleep when traveling.

5. Write the name of the store where you could shop.

Keys to Legibility Score Box		
Check:	**Satisfactory**	**Needs to Improve**
size	☐	☐
shape	☐	☐
slant	☐	☐
spacing	☐	☐
smoothness	☐	☐

13

O O _ _ _ _ _ _ _ _ O

O _ _ _ _ _ _ _ _

onions _____ _____ _____

oranges _____ _____

O O _ _ _ _ _ _ _ _ O

O _ _ _ _ _ _ _ _

October _____

Otto picked oranges.

O O _ _ _ _ _ _

aA

Trace and write.

a a _ _ _ _ _ _ _ _ _ a

a _ _ _ _ _ _ _ _ _ _

apples _ _ _ _ _ _ _ _

pancakes _ _ _ _ _ _ _

A A _ _ _ _ _ _ _ _ A

A _ _ _ _ _ _ _

Alabama _ _ _ _ _ _

Anna _ _ _ _ _

a _ _ _ _ A

Write directions for making pancakes.

d D

Trace and write.

d d _ _ _ _ _ _ d

d _ _ _ _ _ _ _ _

dentist _____ _____

doctor _____ _____

D D _ _ _ _ _ _ _ D

D _ _ _ _ _ _ _ _ _

Deidra _____ _____

Dr. Dodd _____

d _ _ _ D _ _ _ _

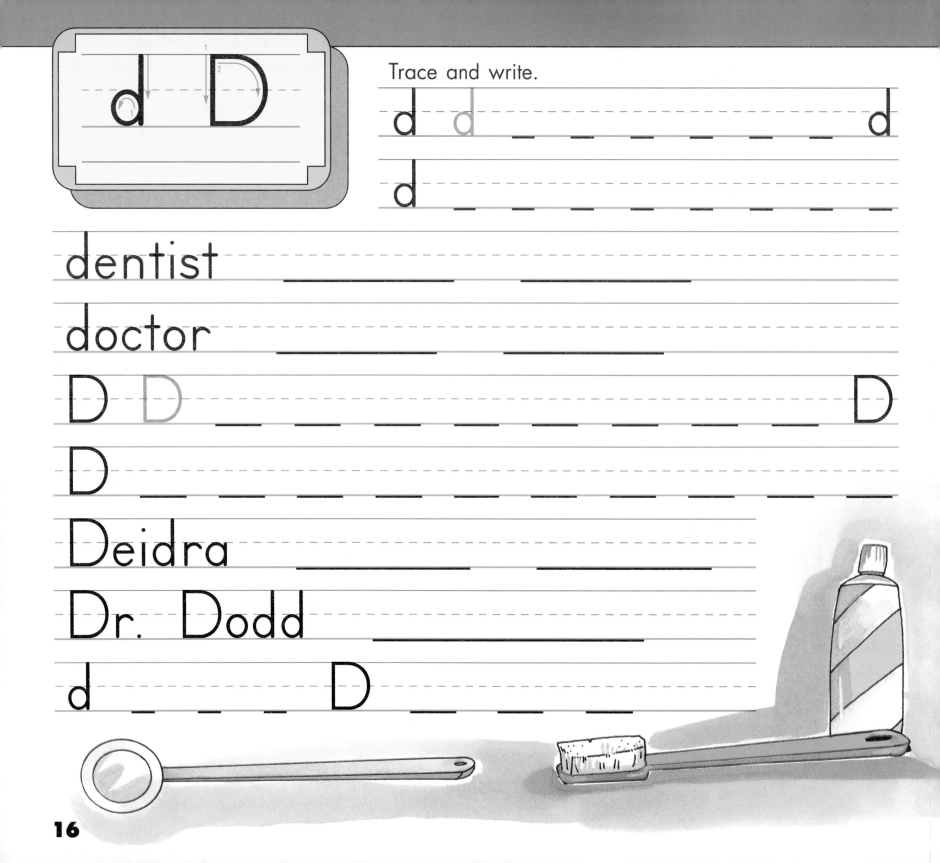

c C

C C _ _ _ _ _ _ _ C

C _ _ _ _ _ _ _

careful _____ _____

chance _____ _____

C C _ _ _ _ _ _ _ C

C _ _ _ _ _ _ _

Colorado _____

Chuck _____ _____

c C _ _ _ _ _

Tell why you think Chuck likes his eye doctor.

Checkpoint My letters are the correct size. ☐ Yes ☐ No

17

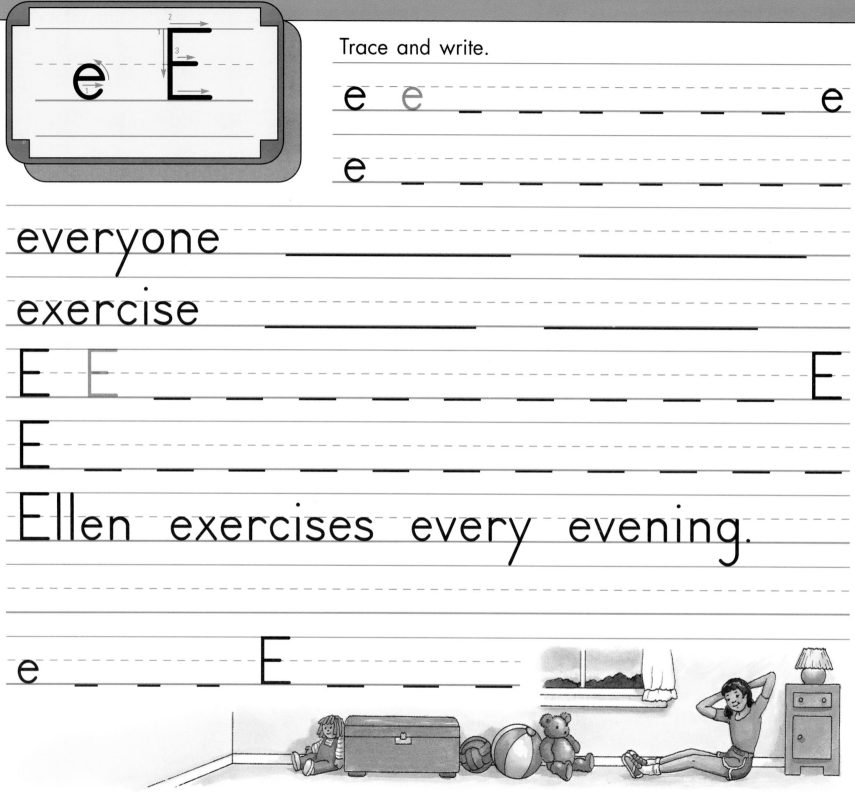

Trace and write.

e   e   e   e

e

everyone

exercise

E   E   E

E

Ellen exercises every evening.

e   E

f F

f

Trace and write.

f f _ _ _ _ _ _ f

f _ _ _ _ _ _

fruit _ _ _ _ _

fresh _ _ _ _ _

F F _ _ _ _ F

F _ _ _ _ _

Fred's fish

f _ _ _ F _ _

Checkpoint My letters are smooth. ☐ **Yes** ☐ **No**

Look at the picture and write a story about what you see.

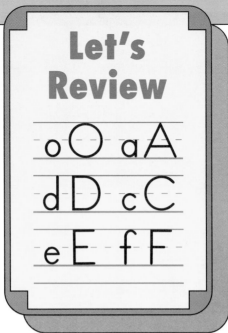

oO aA

dD cC

eE fF

As asphalt and concrete
Replace bushes and trees,
As highways and buildings
Replace marshes and woods,
What will replace
The song of the birds?

Tony Chen

Write the poem.

Endangered Animals

California condor	cheetah	Asian elephant
Eskimo curlew	eagle	Florida panther

Write the names in alphabetical order.

1. _____

2. _____

3. _____

4. _____

5. _____

6. _____

Keys to Legibility Score Box		
Check:	Satisfactory	Needs to Improve
size	☐	☐
shape	☐	☐
slant	☐	☐
spacing	☐	☐
smoothness	☐	☐

g G

g g _ _ _ _ _ _ g

g _ _ _ _

grapes _____ _

geography _____

G G G _ _ _ _ _ G

G _ _ _ _ _ _ _

Grapes grow in Greece.

g _ _ _ G _ _ _

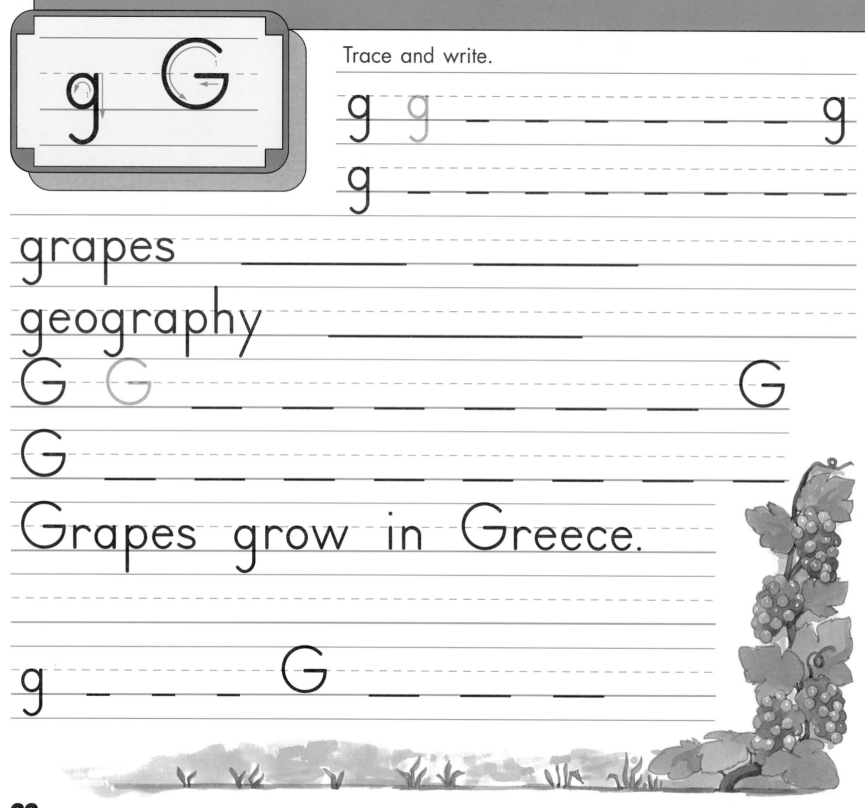

22

j J

Trace and write.

j j j

j

jet

joyful

j j J

J

Japan

Julie and Jerry

j J

23

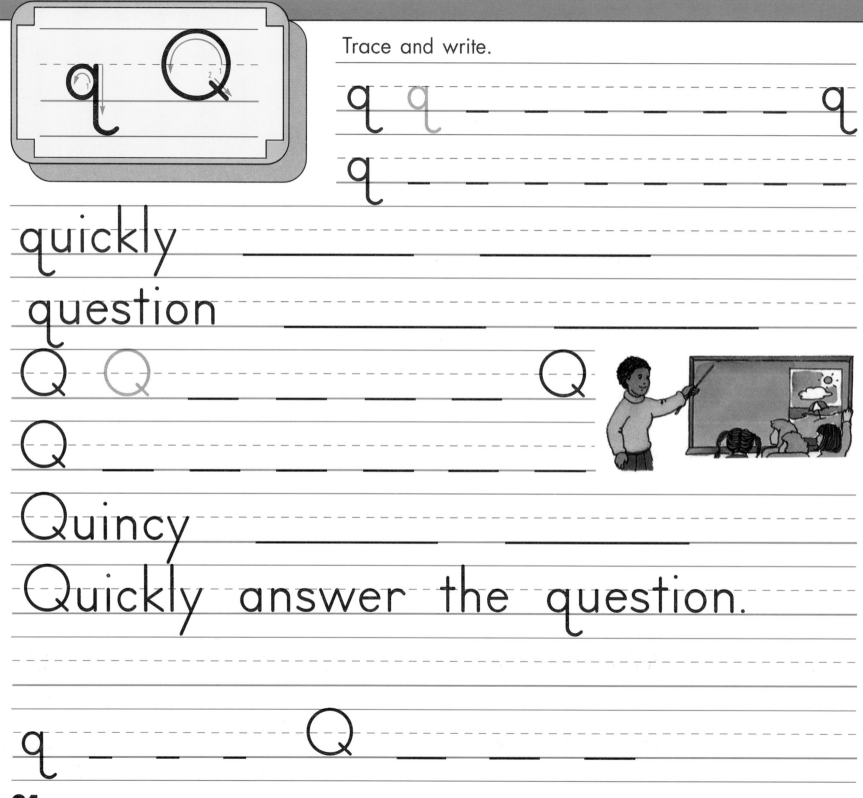

q Q

q q _ _ _ _ _ q

q _ _ _ _ _ _

quickly _____ _____

question _____ _____

Q Q _ _ _ _ Q

Q _ _ _ _ _

Quincy _____ _____

Quickly answer the question.

q _ _ _ Q _ _ _

24

u U

u u _ _ _ _ _ _ _ u

u _ _ _ _ _ _ _

under _____

umbrella _____

U U _ _ _ _ _ _ _ U

U _ _ _ _ _ _ _

Ursula _____

Use the umbrella.

u _ _ _ U _ _ _

Checkpoint My spacing is correct. ☐ Yes ☐ No

25

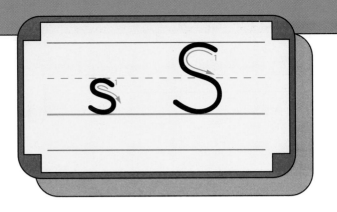

Trace and write.

s   s _ _ _ _ _ _ _   s

s _ _ _ _ _ _ _

sees _____ _____ _____

crossing _____ _____

S   S _ _ _ _ _ _ _   S

S _ _ _ _ _ _ _

Steve looks both ways.

s _ _ _ S _ _ _

Write a list of safety rules.

b B

Trace and write.

b b _____ b

b _____

baseball _____ _____

basketball _____ _____

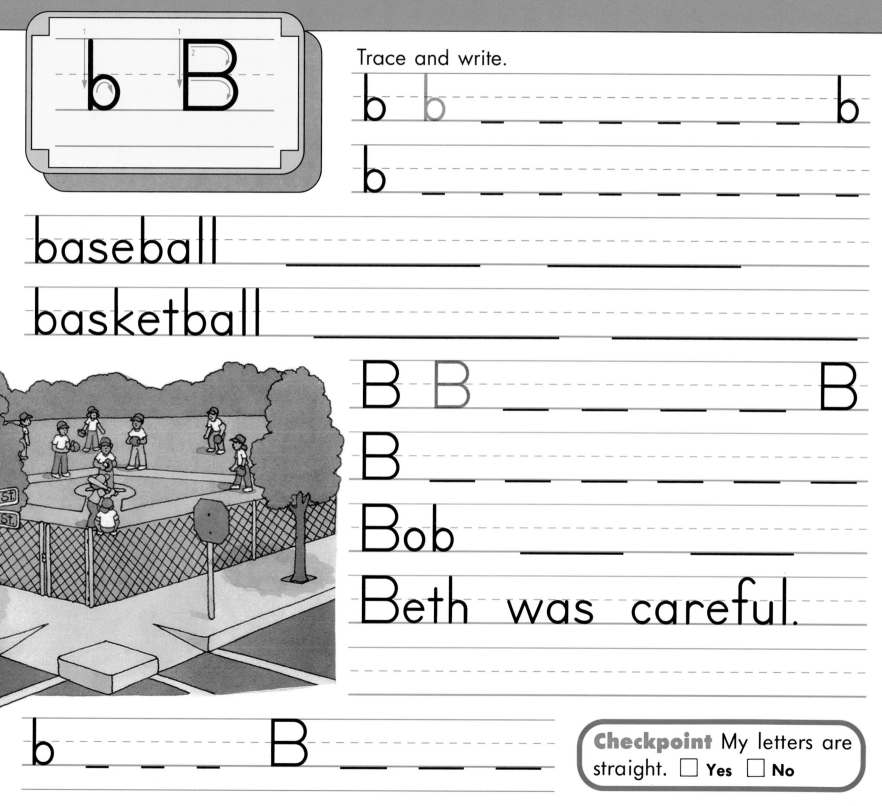

B B _____ B

B _____

Bob _____ _____

Beth was careful.

b _____ B _____

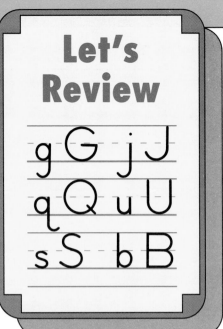

g G j J
q Q u U
s S b B

Add words. Write the complete sentences.

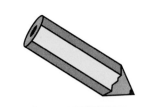

Gus can smell

Quinn tasted

Sally felt

Ursula heard

28

John and Bob saw

Write the sense you use beside each picture.

Keys to Legibility Score Box		
Check:	**Satisfactory**	**Needs to Improve**
size	☐	☐
shape	☐	☐
slant	☐	☐
spacing	☐	☐
smoothness	☐	☐

p P

Trace and write.

p p _ _ _ _ _ _ _ p

p _ _ _ _ _ _

please _____ _____

paper _____ _____

P P _ _ _ _ _ _ _ P

P _ _ _ _ _ _

Pick up the paper.

Pepper _____

p P _ _ _ _ _

Checkpoint My letters are the correct size. ☐ Yes ☐ No

30

r R

Trace and write.

r r _ _ _ _ _ r

r _ _ _ _ _

river _ _ _

farther _ _

R R R _ _ _ R

R _ _ _ _

Rivers run deep.

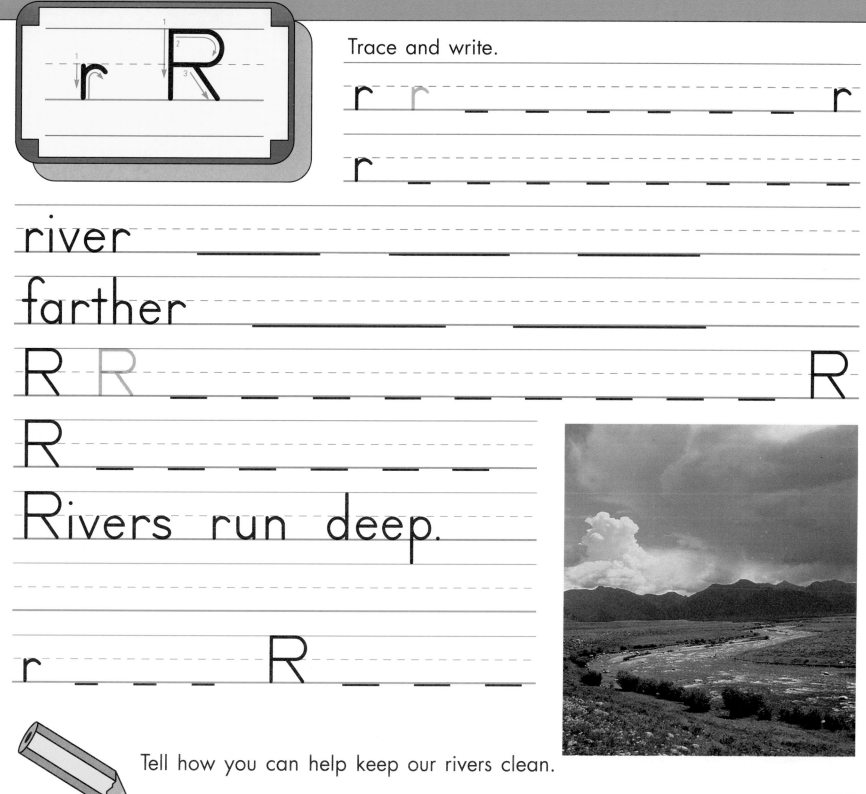

r r _ _ R _ _

Tell how you can help keep our rivers clean.

n N

Trace and write.

n n _ _ _ _ _ _ _ n

n _ _ _ _ _ _ _ _

nine _ _ _ _ _ _

planets _ _ _ _

N N _ _ _ _ _ _ N

N _ _ _ _ _ _ _

Neptune _ _ _ _

North Star _ _ _ _

n N _ _ _ _

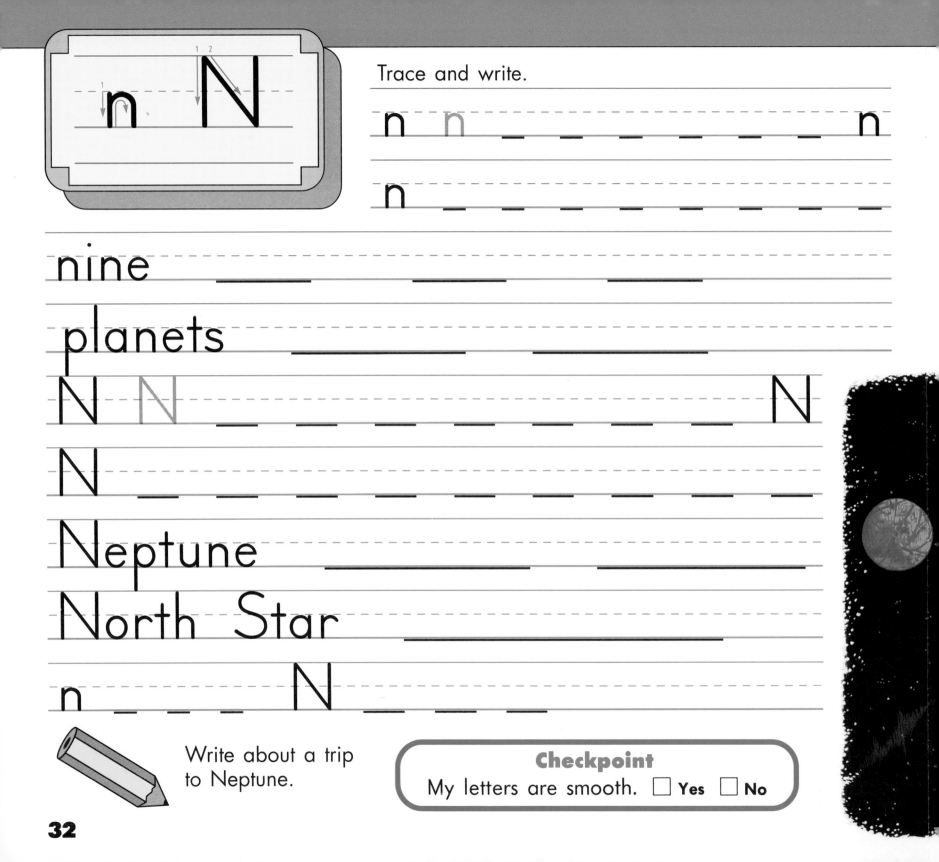

Write about a trip to Neptune.

Checkpoint
My letters are smooth. ☐ Yes ☐ No

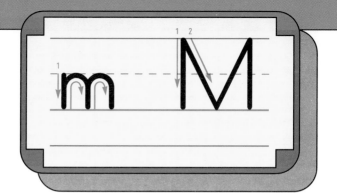

m M

Trace and write.

m　m　＿　＿　＿　m

m　＿　＿　＿

moons　＿　＿

millions　＿　＿

M M ＿＿＿ M

M ＿＿＿

Mercury ＿＿＿

Mars has two moons.

m ＿＿ M ＿＿

h H

Trace and write.

h   h   _ _ _ _   h

h   _ _ _ _ _ _

hush   _ _ _   _ _ _   _ _ _

hurry   _ _ _ _   _ _ _ _   _ _ _

H H   _ _ _ _ _ _ _ _ _   H

H   _ _ _   _ _ _   _ _ _

Harold   _ _ _ _

Helen hurried home.

_ _ _ _ _ _ _ _ _ _ _ _

h   _ _ _   H   _ _ _ _ _ _

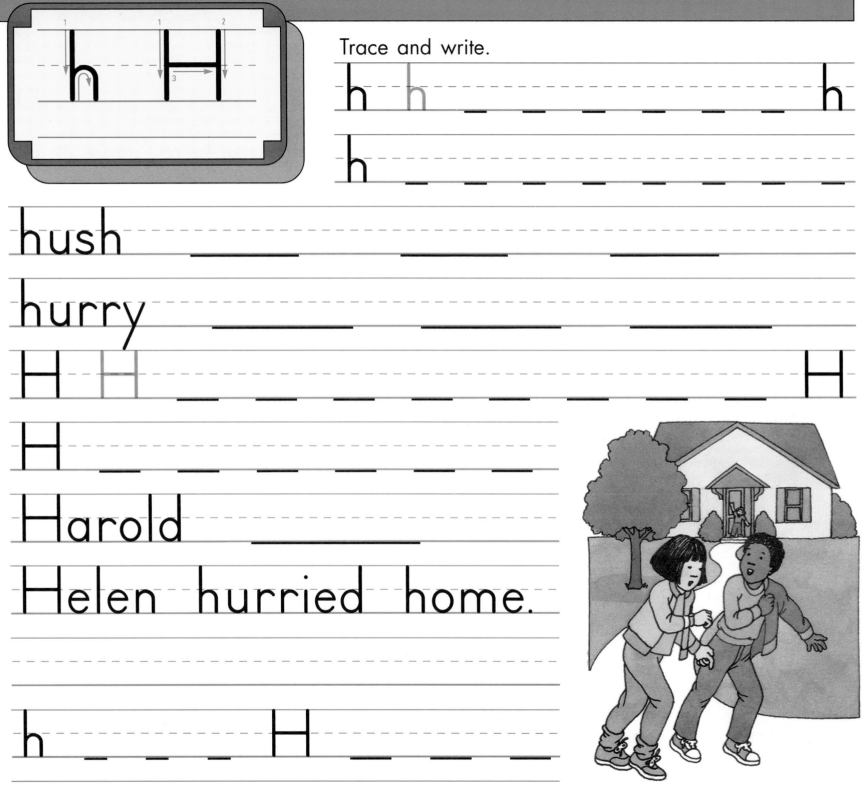

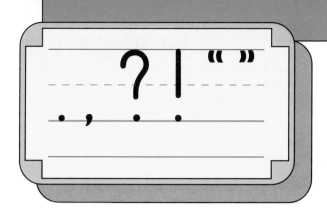

Punctuation Marks

Punctuate the sentences below. Then write the sentences with the punctuation marks.

1. Ralph asked What time is it

2. It is time to go

3. Walk faster Luci called

4. Will we be home in time

1. _____

2. _____

3. _____

4. _____

Let's Review

pPrR
nNmM
hH

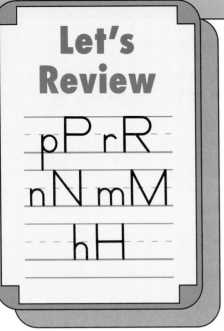

Find a name in the box that rhymes with each name below. Write the rhyming name.

Ramona	Patty	Mandy
Harry	Nina	Capp
Robbie	Ryan	Ron
Juanita	Phil	Kim

Juan _____

Regina _____

Rita _____

Brian _____

Bill _____

Bobby _____

Tim _____

Mary _____

Nap _____

Nona _____

Mattie _____

Randi _____

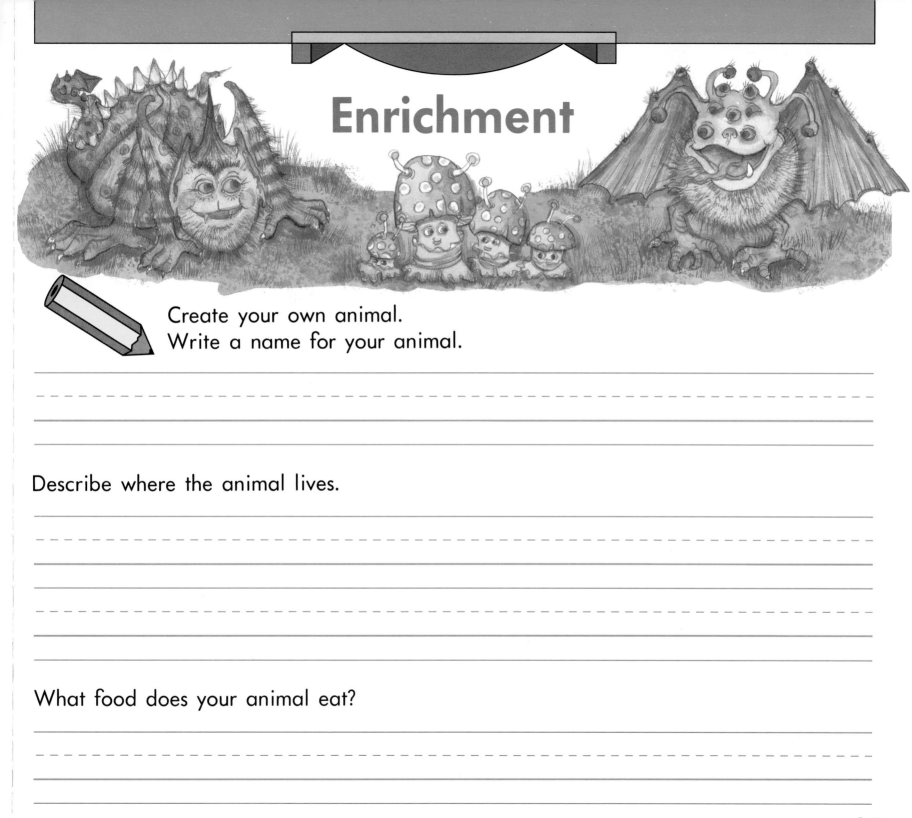

Enrichment

Create your own animal.
Write a name for your animal.

Describe where the animal lives.

What food does your animal eat?

V V   V

V

vine

vegetable

V V   V

V

Vivian

Van's vegetables

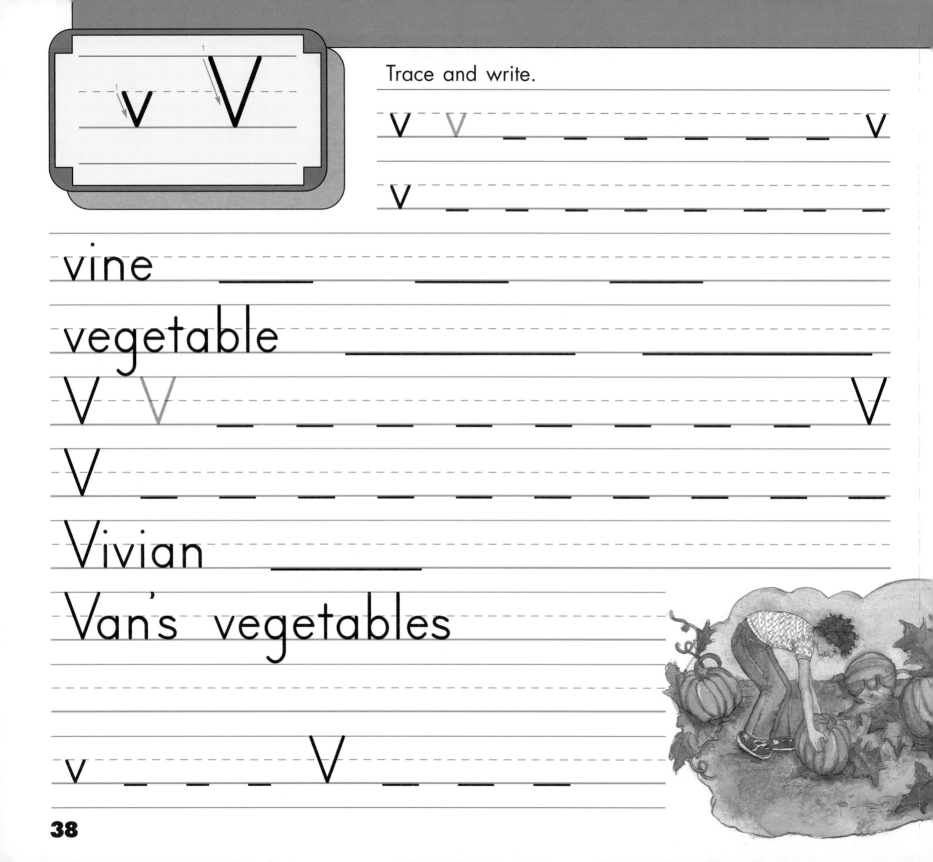

v   V

38

y Y

y y — — — — — y

y — — —

young

yellow

Y Y — — — — — Y

Y — — — — —

Yolanda

y — — —

Y — — —

39

w W

Trace and write.

W W _ _ _ _ _ W

W _ _ _ _ _ _ _

weather _____ _____

wonderful _____ _____

W W _____ _____ W

W _ _ _ _ _

William _____

Where is the rainbow?

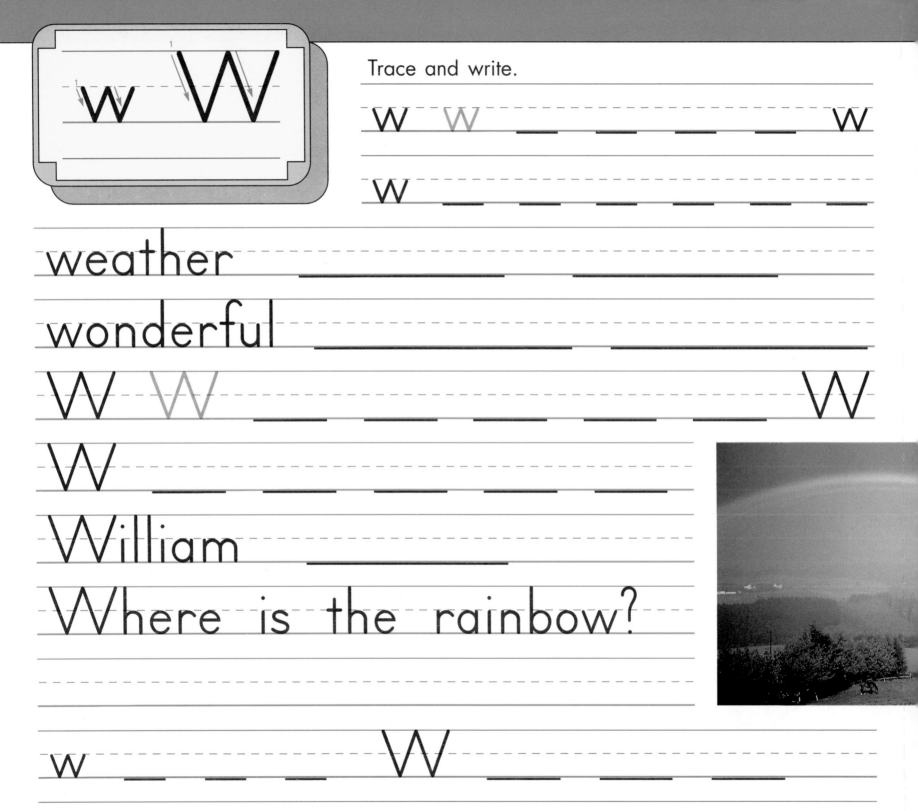

w _ _ _ W _ _ _

k K

k k _ _ _ _ _ _ _ k

k _ _ _ _ _ _ _ _

kick _ _ _ _ _ _

knock _ _ _ _ _ _

K K _ _ _ _ _ _ _ K

K _ _ _ _ _ _ _ _

Kevin _ _ _ _

Kay looked for the end.

k _ _ _ K _ _ _ _

Checkpoint My letters are straight. ☐ **Yes** ☐ **No**

41

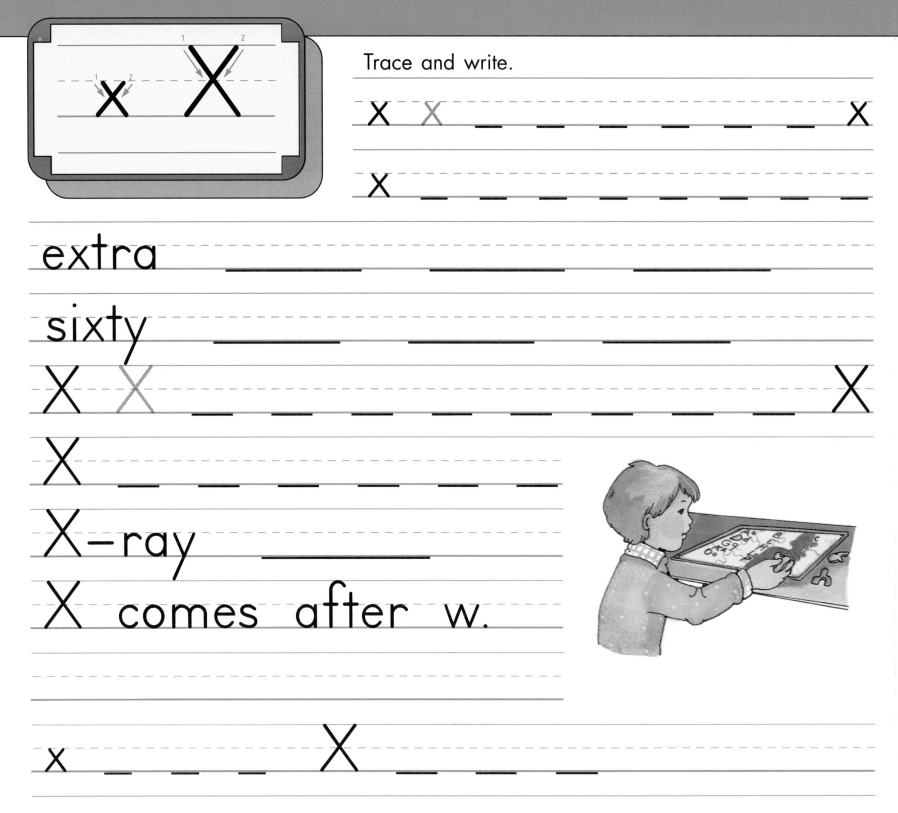

Trace and write.

X X X _____ X

X _____

extra _____

sixty _____

X X _____ X

X _____

X-ray _____

X comes after w.

x _____ X _____

z Z

Trace and write.

z z _____ z

z _____

zoom _____

zero _____

Z Z _____ Z

Z _____

Zelda's puzzle won the prize.

Zola _____

z ____ Z _____

Let's Review

vV yY
wW kK
xX zZ

Newspaper headlines tell the story.

Kind People Give Extra Help

Whales Get Trapped in Ice

Yukon River is Frozen

Write the headline that goes with the picture.

1.

2.

3.

1. _____

2. _____

3. _____

Manuscript Posttest

Write the first verse. Use your best manuscript handwriting.

Look in a Book

Look in a book
and you will see
words and magic
and mystery.

Look in a book
and you will find
sense and nonsense
of every kind.

Look in a book
and you will know
all the things that
can help you grow.

Ivy O. Eastwick

Keys to Legibility Score Box		
Check:	**Satisfactory**	**Needs to Improve**
size	☐	☐
shape	☐	☐
slant	☐	☐
spacing	☐	☐
smoothness	☐	☐

Introduction to Cursive

A New Friend

They've taken in the furniture;
I watched them carefully.
I wondered, "Will there be a child
Just right to play with me?"

So I peeked through the garden fence
(I couldn't wait to see).
I found the little boy next door
Was peeking back at me.

Marjorie Allen Anderson

Lowercase Cursive Letters

Match the manuscript to cursive.

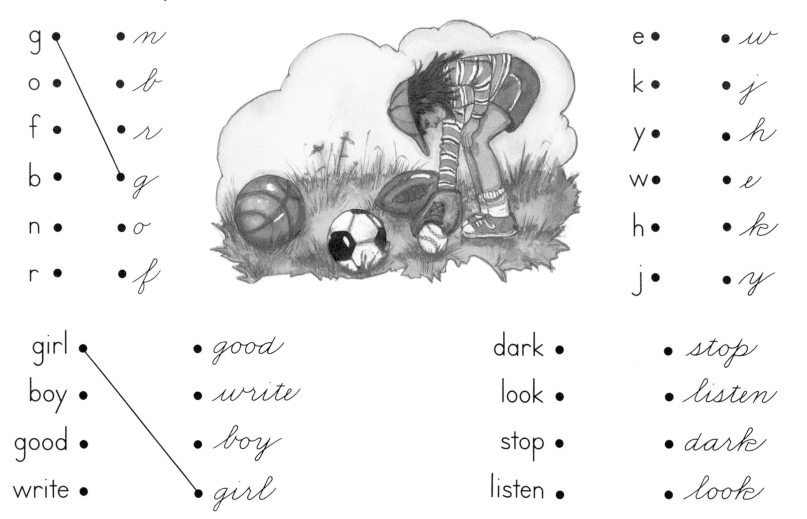

g •   • *n*
o •   • *b*
f •   • *r*
b •   • *g*
n •   • *o*
r •   • *f*

e •   • *w*
k •   • *j*
y •   • *h*
w •   • *e*
h •   • *k*
j •   • *y*

girl •   • *good*
boy •   • *write*
good •   • *boy*
write •   • *girl*

dark •   • *stop*
look •   • *listen*
stop •   • *dark*
listen •   • *look*

Look at these two words. How are they different?

basketball   *basketball*

Uppercase Cursive Letters

Match the manuscript to cursive.

B •   • 𝒶

D •   • 𝒮

N •   • ℬ

E •   • 𝓃

A •   • 𝒟

S •   • ℰ

Lisa •   • Heather

Sean •   • Chad

Ryan •   • Lisa

Todd •   • Sean

Heather •   • Michael

Chad •   • Ryan

Michael •   • Todd

Ingrid •   • Nancy

Debbie •   • Ingrid

Carlos •   • Sue

Nancy •   • David

Rosa •   • Debbie

David •   • Carlos

Sue •   • Rosa

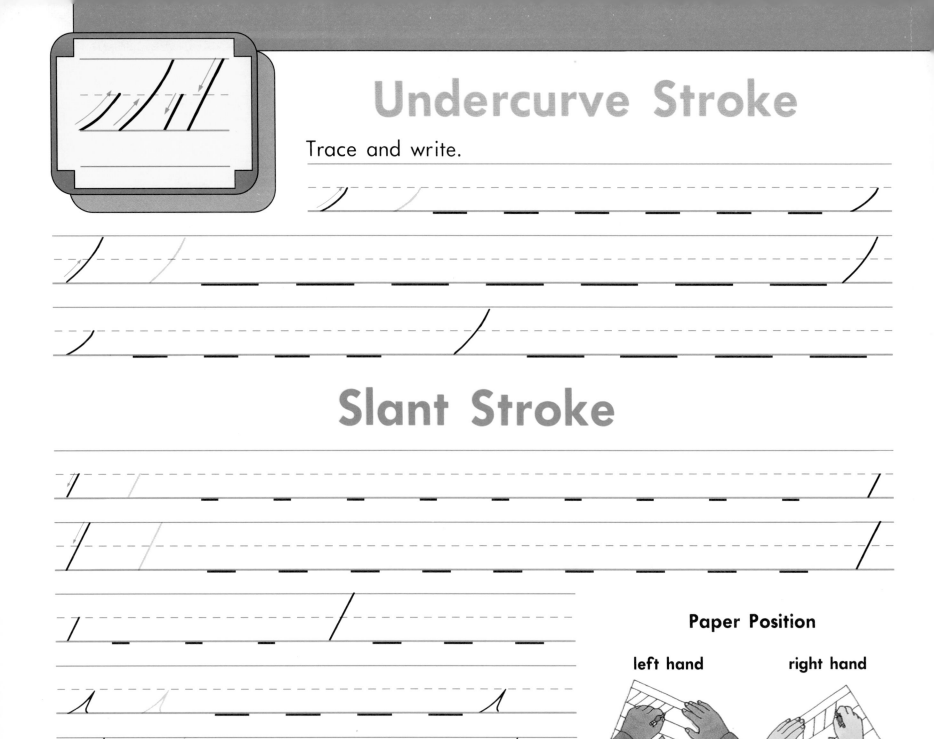

Undercurve Stroke

Trace and write.

Slant Stroke

Paper Position

left hand   right hand

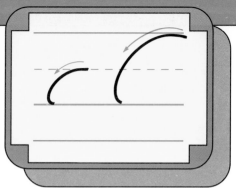

Downcurve Stroke

Trace and write.

Find the downcurve in each letter.
Trace the downcurve strokes.

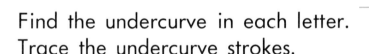

Find the undercurve in each letter.
Trace the undercurve strokes.

Find the slant stroke in each letter.
Trace the slant strokes.

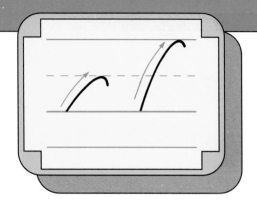

Overcurve Stroke

Trace and write.

Find the overcurve in each letter.
Trace the overcurve strokes.

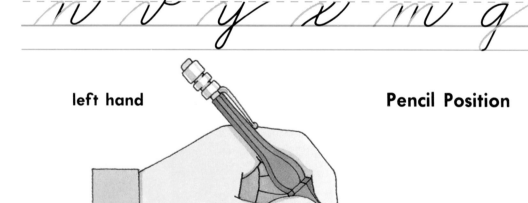

left hand　　　　**Pencil Position**　　　　**right hand**

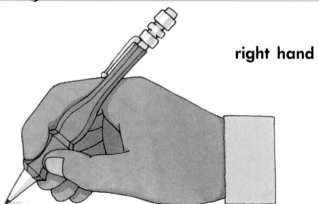

Checkstroke

Trace and write.

Find the checkstroke in each letter.
Trace the checkstrokes.

$b \ o \ v \ w$

Write the following strokes.

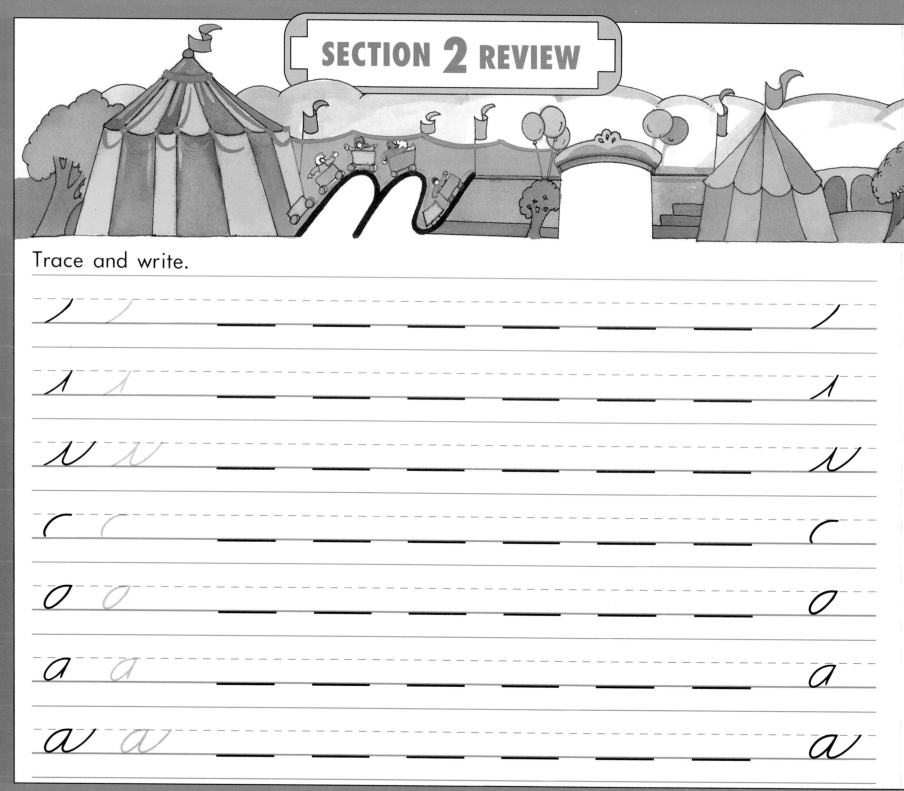

Trace and write.

Trace and write.

Checkpoint

My basic strokes ☐ **are satisfactory.** ☐ **need improvement.**

Undercurve Beginnings

Just Me

Nobody sees what I can see,
For back of my eyes there is only me.
And nobody knows how my thoughts begin,
For there's only myself inside my skin.
Isn't it strange how everyone owns
Just enough skin to cover his bones?
My father's would be too big to fit—
I'd be all wrinkled inside of it.
And my baby brother's is much too small—
It just wouldn't cover me up at all.
But I feel just right in the skin I wear,
And there's nobody like me anywhere.

Margaret Hillert

Trace and write.

i

i *i* *i*

i

Undercurve Joining

ii ii

i

left hand **Paper Position** **right hand**

Pull toward left elbow. Pull toward midsection.

You're Invited

Trace and write.

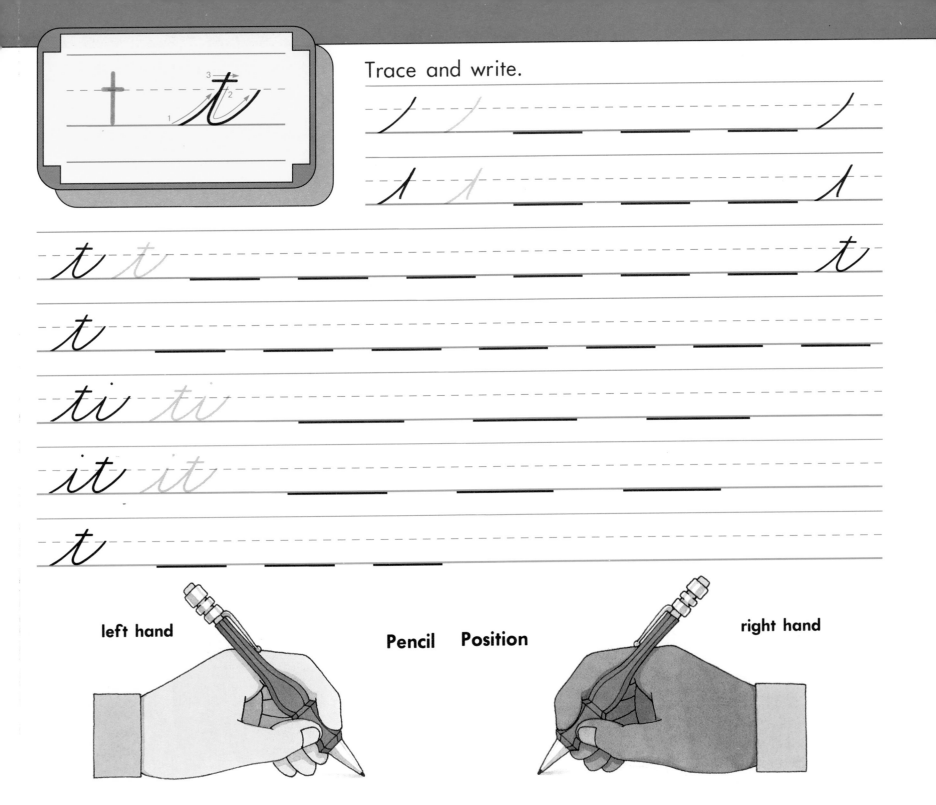

left hand

Pencil   Position

right hand

u

Trace and write.

u u _____ _____ u

u u _____ _____ u

u _____ _____ _____ _____

ut ut _____ _____ _____

uit uit _____ _____

tiu tiu _____ _____

utu utu _____ _____ _____

u _____ _____ _____

Checkpoint
Do your ending strokes end at the midline? ☐ **Yes** ☐ **No**

tulips

60

W W w

Trace and write.

w w _____ _____ w

w w _____ _____ w

w , _____ _____ _____ _____ _____

w _____ _____ _____ _____ w

Checkstroke Joining

wi wi _____ _____

wit wit _____ _____

twi twi _____ _____

wu wu _____ _____

w _____ _____ _____

flowers

61

e ℓ

Trace and write.

ℓ ℓ ℓ

ℓ ℓ ℓ

ℓ ℓ

ℓ ℓ

et et

wet wet

we we

tie tie

ℓ

i t u

w e

tweet

Write each joining two times and underline the best joining.

ti _____ _____

te _____ _____

wi _____ _____

we _____ _____

twu _____ _____

Write each word three times and underline the best one.

tweet _____ _____ _____

tee _____ _____ _____

Checkpoint My undercurve joinings
☐ **are satisfactory.** ☐ **need improvement.**

Trace and write.

l l l l

l l l l

l l l

l

lit

will

wilt

tell

tile

l

Checkpoint
Did you close the loop in **l** at the midline? ☐ **Yes** ☐ **No**

b _b_

Trace and write.

_b_ _b_ _b_

_b_ _b_ _b_

_b_ _b_ _b_

_b_

_be_ _be_

_bi_

_bu_

built

belt

_b_

65

h h

l *l* _____ _____ *l*

l *l* _____ _____ *l*

h *h* _____ _____ _____ *h*

h _____ _____ _____

he _____ _____ *heel* _____

hu _____ _____ *hut* _____

hi _____ _____ *hill* _____

the hub _____

the wheel _____

h _____ _____

Checkpoint
My undercurves ☐ **are satisfactory.**
☐ **need to improve.**

66

Trace and write.

k k k k

k k k

k

k k

ki   kite

ke   kettle

hike

week

the bike

k

67

Let's Review

l b

h k

Rhyming Words

I like to look
Inside a book.

bell   but   bee   bill   like   blew
kite   while   kit   let   belt   built

Write a word from the box that rhymes with each word below.

flew _____   wet _____   hike _____

hit _____   see _____   melt _____

cut _____   white _____   mile _____

well _____   hill _____   quilt _____

Checkpoint
- ☐ My letters are formed correctly.
- ☐ My letters need to improve.

Manuscript Maintenance

Tongue Twisters

Three tiny toads traveled to town.

Four flies flew from the fresh flowers.

Many men marched to market.

Bill bought bread and butter.

Write in manuscript the tongue twister you like best.

Write a tongue twister of your own.

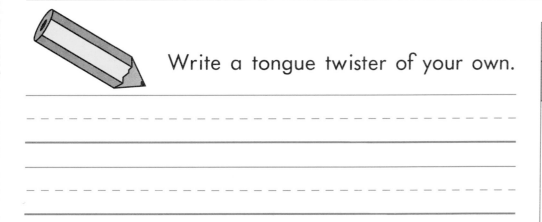

Keys to Legibility Score Box		
Check:	Satisfactory	Needs to Improve
size	☐	☐
shape	☐	☐
slant	☐	☐
spacing	☐	☐
smoothness	☐	☐

r r

Trace and write.

r r   r

r   r

r

ri _____ write _____

ru _____ ruler _____

write the rule

r

School Rules
1. No running
2. Obey al

Write a list of school rules.

S s

Trace and write.

/

s

s

s

sh   shirt

str   strike

sw   sweet

sells shirts

s

f

Trace and write.

f *f*   *f*

f *f*   *f*

f *f*   *f*

f

fr   *free*

fu   *full*

fresh fruit

f

Write about your favorite fruit.

p

Trace and write.

1 1 — — 1

1 1 — — 1

p p — — p

p p — — p

p — —

pu — —   pup —

spi — —   spill —

free puppies

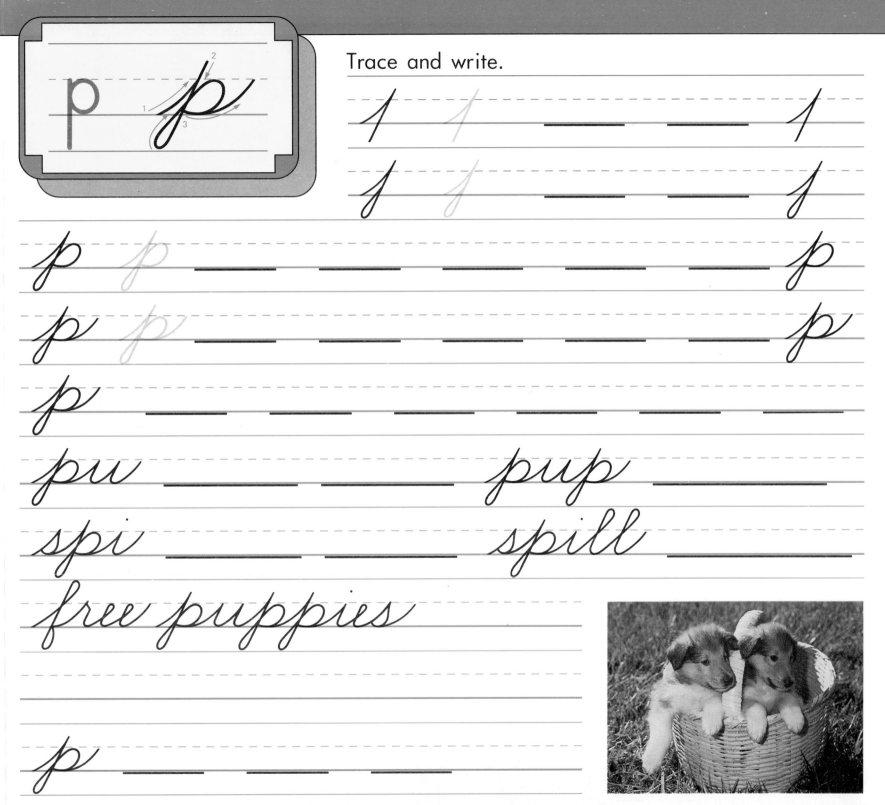

p — —

Trace and write.

j   j   j   j

j   j   j   j

j

j   j

Overcurve Joining   je   je   jet

ju   just

jeep

jewels

j

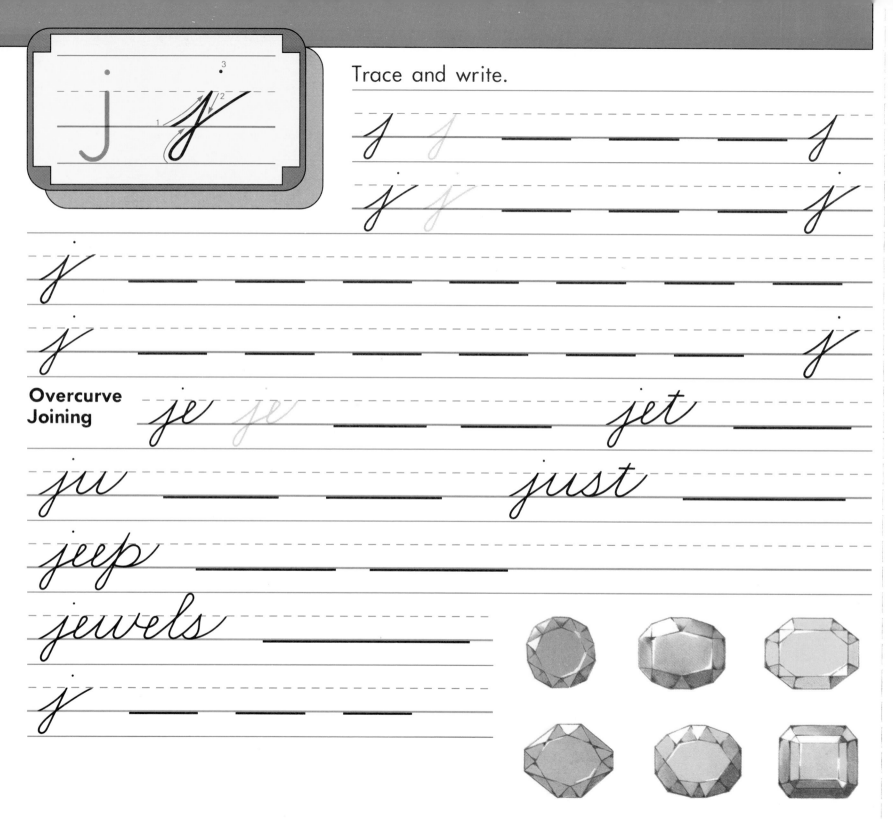

74

Let's Review

r s f

p j

Means the Same

jet   street
trip   field   slept

Read each sentence. Read the underlined word.
Choose the word in the box that means the same as the underlined word. Write it in the space.

1. We took a <u>vacation</u> in Chicago.

2. The car went down the <u>road</u>.

3. The cow is in the <u>meadow</u>.

4. He <u>napped</u> in the chair.

Checkpoint

My slant ☐ **is satisfactory.**
☐ **needs to improve.**

5. Carol flew in a <u>plane</u>.

75

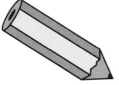

Manuscript Maintenance

Finish the story in manuscript.

I am happy when

Write the words that sound the same.

peel hi here write heel

there sell week blue threw

right	heal
cell	high
blew	weak
peal	hear
through	their

Downcurve Beginnings

Don't Ever Cross A Crocodile

Don't ever cross a crocodile
However few his faults.
Don't ever dare
A dancing bear
To teach you how to waltz.

Don't ever poke a rattlesnake
Who's sleeping in the sun
And say the poke
Was just a joke
And really all in fun.

Don't ever lure a lion close
With gifts of steak and suet.
Though lion-looks
Are nice in books
Don't ever, ever do it.

Kaye Starbird

a *a*

C   C _____ _____ _____   C

O   O _____ _____ _____   O

a   a _____ _____ _____   a

a   a _____ _____ _____   a

a _____ _____ _____ _____

ai _____ _____ pail _____

aw _____ _____ awhile _____

a salt shaker

a _____ _____

80

d

d d   d

d d   d

d d   d

d

di   did

da da

date   dress

leader

parade

d

81

g g

Trace and write.

g   g   ___ ___ ___   g

g   g   ___ ___ ___   g

g   g   ___ ___ ___   g

g   ___ ___ ___

ge   ge   ___ ___   gear   ___

ga   ga   ___ ___   gas   ___

big garage

large gate

g   ___ ___ ___

q q

q q _ _ _ q

q q _ _ _ q

q _ _ _ _

qu _ _ quiet _

quart _ _

quarter _ _

quite a quilt

q _ _

O O   O

O O   O

O

O   O

or or ___   ow ow ___

alligator ___   owl ___

oa oa ___   oo oo ___

toad ___

rooster ___

o ___

C C

Trace and write.

C C   C

C C   C

C

C   C

cu   cub

ca   cat

ick   chick

crocodile

cricket

C

Write a conversation
between the rooster
and the chick.

85

Manuscript Maintenance

Friendly Letter

Dear Ryan,

    Could you and Heather come to visit me?

We will go to the beach every day.

Todd

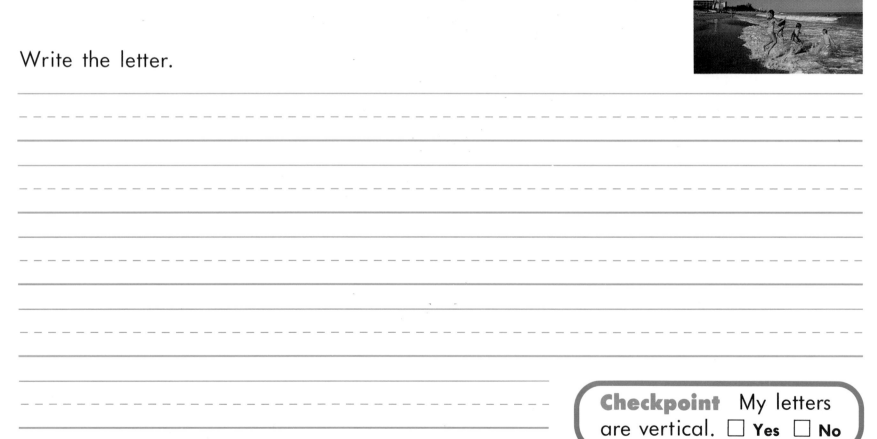

Write the letter.

Checkpoint My letters are vertical. ☐ Yes ☐ No

adgqoc

SECTION 4 REVIEW

Opposites

Write a word that means the opposite of each word below. Use the words in the box.

close	quiet	below	take
cold	after	good	dark

1. loud _____

2. before _____

3. hot _____

4. open _____

5. light _____

6. above _____

7. give _____

8. bad _____

Checkpoint
☐ My letters are satisfactory.
☐ My letters need to improve.

Overcurve Beginnings

Butterfly Wings

How would it be
on a day in June
to open your eyes
in a dark cocoon,

And soften one end
and crawl outside,
and find you had wings
to open wide,

And find you could fly
to a bush or tree
or float on the air
like a boat at sea . . .

How would it be?

Aileen Fisher

n *n*

n n n   n

m m m   m

m m   m

m

ni ni   nine

nc nc   inch

nn nn   inn

drinking fountain

m

m /m

m   m   m

m   m   m

m   m   m

m

mi   mileage

ma   machine

om   om   home

measure

rooms

m

91

Trace and write.

$\mathcal{V}$ $\mathcal{V}$ $\mathcal{V}$

$\mathcal{N}$ $\mathcal{N}$ $\mathcal{N}$

$\mathcal{N}$

$\mathcal{N}$ $\mathcal{N}$

vi   village

overhead

evening

travel

van

$\mathcal{N}$

$\mathcal{X}$

$\mathcal{N}$ $\mathcal{N}$ $\mathcal{N}$ _____ _____ _____ $\mathcal{N}$

$\mathcal{X}$ $\mathcal{X}$ _____ _____ _____ $\mathcal{X}$

x _____ _____ _____ _____ _____

x _____ _____ _____ _____ x

xi _____ _____ $exit$ _____

xt _____ _____ $extra$ _____

$foxes$ _____ _____

$explore$ _____

$axes$ _____

x _____ _____

y y

y y

y

y

ye *yellow*

ya *yard*

ym *gym*

everybody

plays

y

Z

z

z

z

z

ze maze

zo zoom

za

zigzag

z

95

Numerals

Trace and write.

1   1 _____ _____

2   2 _____ _____

3   3 _____ _____

4   4 _____ _____

5   5 _____ _____

6   6 _____ _____

7   7 _____ _____

8   8 _____ _____

9   9 _____ _____

10   10 _____ _____

Write the numerals 1 through 10.

Write the numerals 10 through 1.

96

n m v
x y z

Language Arts

Think of a dictionary as having three parts.

Choose three words you would find beginning with the letters A-F.

Choose three words you would find beginning with the letters G-P.

Choose three words you would find beginning with the letters Q-Z.

valley   exercise
monkey   zoom
number   breeze
anyone   heavy
summer

Write the words in alphabetical order in the appropriate column.

A-F	G-P	Q-Z

Checkpoint ☐ My letter size is satisfactory.
☐ My letter size needs to improve.

Backward Oval and Overcurve Loop Letters

The Elephant's Trunk

A little boy that I know
(He is only six)
Went to find an elephant;
He thought he'd teach it tricks.

But when he found an elephant,
It seemed—to his surprise—
As though its skin had gotten wet
And stretched a bigger size.

He wondered what would happen
If, instead, the skin had shrunk;
Would the elephant then change it
For a spare suit from his trunk?

A little boy that I know
(He is only six)
Went to find an elephant;
And forgot to teach it tricks.

Irma V. Sanderson

Trace and write.

$\mathcal{O}$ $\mathcal{O}$ $\mathcal{O}$ ___ ___ ___ $\mathcal{O}$

a a a ___ ___ ___ a

a a ___ ___ ___ a

a ___ ___ ___ ___

Audrey ___

April ___

Andy ___

Adela went to Atlanta.

a ___ ___ ___

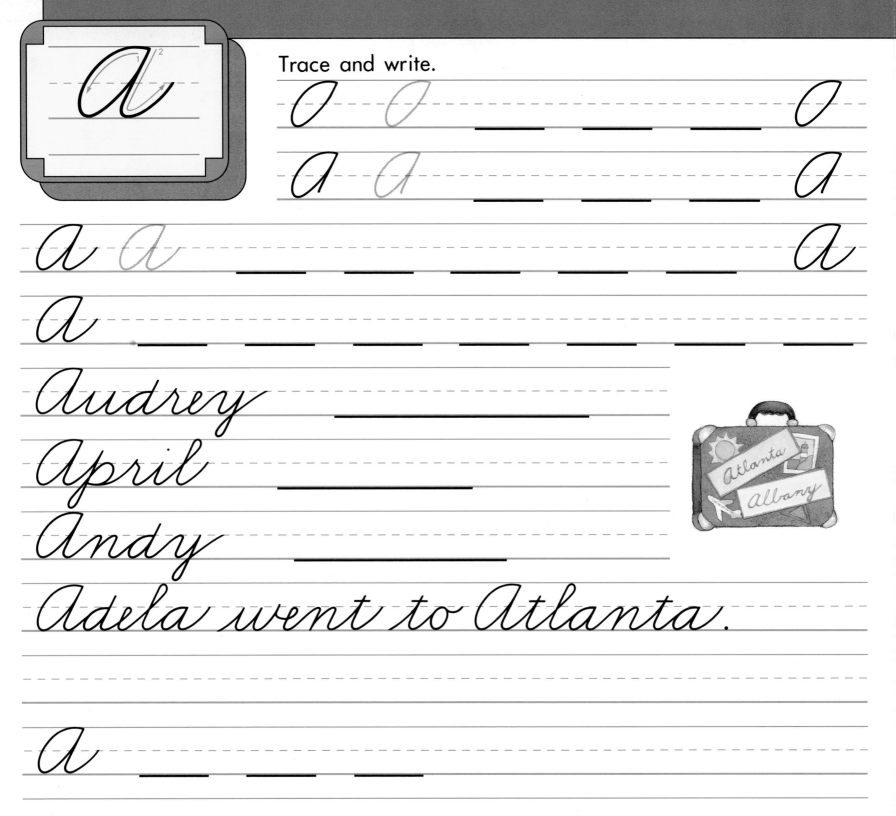

Trace and write.

O O O — — — O

O O O — — — O

O — — — — —

October — —

Oklahoma —

Write this story starter for your own story.

Once upon a time

O — — —

Trace and write.

$\int$ $\int$ $\int$

$\mathcal{D}$ $\mathcal{D}$ $\mathcal{D}$

$\mathcal{D}$ $\mathcal{D}$ $\mathcal{D}$

$\mathcal{D}$

December

Dr. Decker

Don Doring

Detroit

$\mathcal{D}$

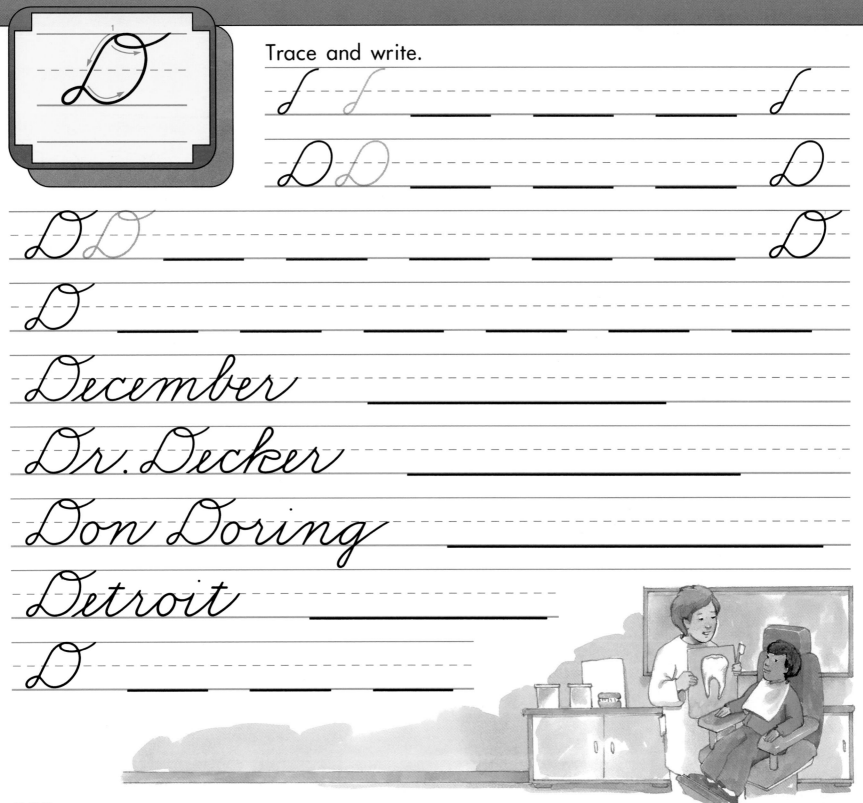

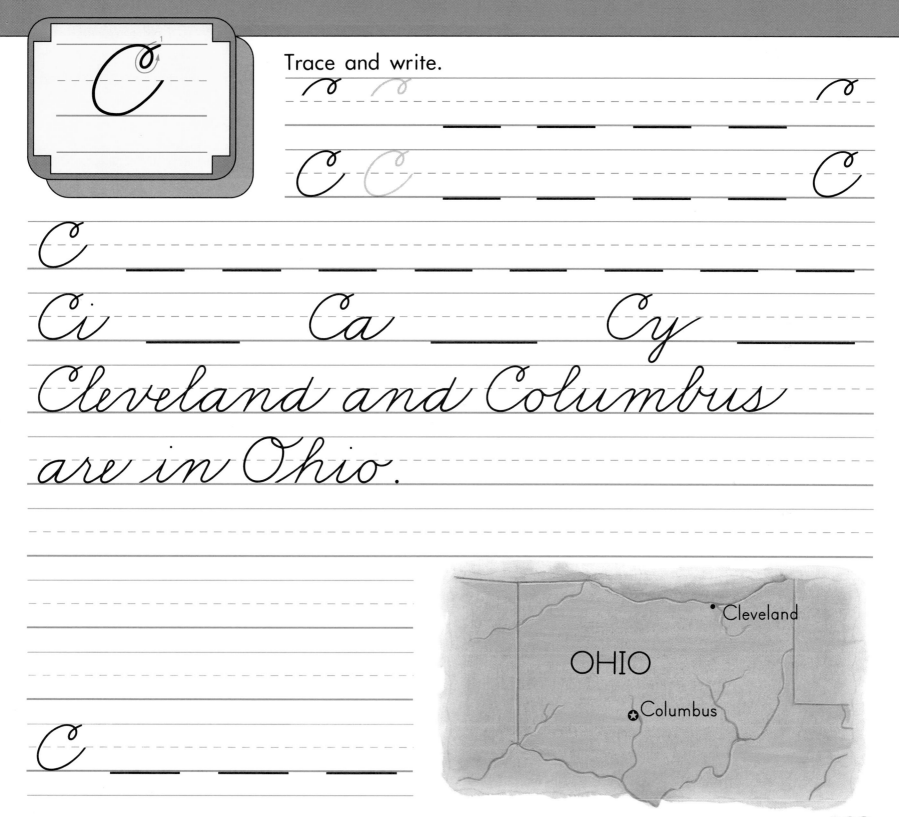

Trace and write.

C C C

C C C

C

Ci   Ca   Cy

Cleveland and Columbus
are in Ohio.

C

OHIO
· Cleveland
★Columbus

$\mathcal{E}$

$\mathcal{E}$ $\mathcal{E}$ $\mathcal{E}$

$\mathcal{E}$ $\mathcal{E}$ $\mathcal{E}$

$\mathcal{E}$

$\mathcal{E}i$ $\mathcal{E}a$ $\mathcal{E}m$

$\mathcal{E}ileen$ $\mathcal{E}arl$

$\mathcal{E}veryone\ enjoyed\ \mathcal{E}mma's$

$party.$

$\mathcal{E}$

Let's Review

a O

D C E

Write the names and addresses.

Carl Camel
95 Onyx Avenue
Chino, CA 91708

Olive Elephant
26 Dairy Avenue
Dover, DE 19901

If you wanted to learn about animals that can go for a long time without water, would you write to Carl or Olive? _____

If you wanted to learn about animals with large trunks, would you write to Carl or Olive? _____

Write a letter to Carl or Olive.

Checkpoint My letters are the correct size. ☐ **Yes** ☐ **No**

Trace and write.

Illinois

Idaho

Indiana

Iowa

Trace and write.

𝒥 𝒥

𝒥 𝒥

𝒥

𝒥 𝒥

Je   Jo

July

January

June

𝒥

Which of these three months
do you like best? Tell why.

107

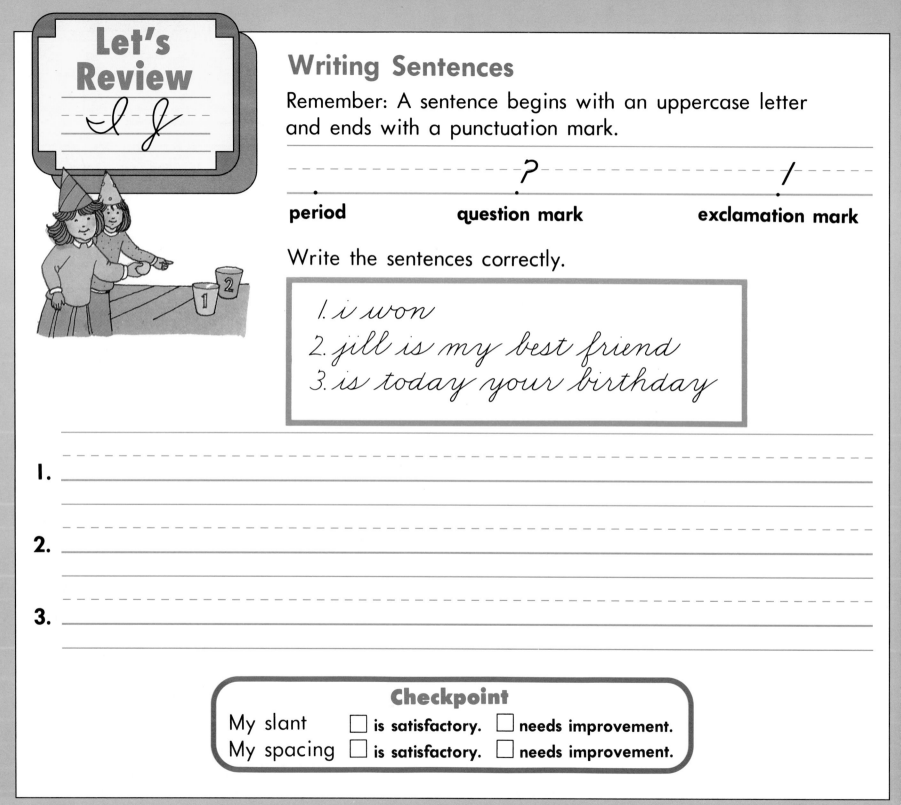

Let's Review

I J

Writing Sentences

Remember: A sentence begins with an uppercase letter and ends with a punctuation mark.

.   ?   !
period   **question mark**   **exclamation mark**

Write the sentences correctly.

> 1. i won
> 2. jill is my best friend
> 3. is today your birthday

1. _____

2. _____

3. _____

Checkpoint

My slant   ☐ is satisfactory. ☐ needs improvement.
My spacing ☐ is satisfactory. ☐ needs improvement.

October 10, 19____

Dear Aunt Ellen,

I want to thank you for the truck you gave me for my birthday. I play with it every day.

Jim

Write the letter from Jim.

Loop Curve Letters

At the Library

This is a lovely place to be.
   The books are everywhere,
And I can read them here, or take
   Them home and read them there.

It is a kind of secret place
   Where I can enter in
And no one tells me where to stop
   Or where I should begin.

The books sit waiting on their shelves,
   As friendly as can be,
And since I am a borrower
   They all belong to me.

Marchette Chute

Trace and write.

$\mathscr{N}$ $\mathscr{N}$

$\mathscr{n}$ $\mathscr{n}$

$\mathscr{n}$

Ne Na Ny

Ned Nora

Nancy's favorite book

is Noisy Nora.

$\mathscr{N}$

Trace and write.

$\mathcal{N}$ $\mathcal{N}$ ____   ____ $\mathcal{N}$

$\mathcal{M}$ $\mathcal{M}$ ____   ____ $\mathcal{M}$

$\mathcal{M}$ ____ ____ ____ ____ ____

$\mathcal{M}$ ____ ____ ____ ____ ____ $\mathcal{M}$

Mi ____ Ma ____ My ____

Mr. Moore read Madeline

to Magda.

$\mathcal{M}$ ____ ____ ____

113

Trace and write.

V V V

U U U

W W W

W

Who's going to Washington, D.C.?

W

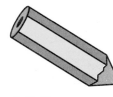

Write about what you would
do in Washington, D.C.

Let's Review
n m w

National Mall
Jefferson Memorial
Washington Monument
Marine Corps War Memorial

List each point of interest in alphabetical order.

1. _____

2. _____

3. _____

4. _____

Checkpoint
My letter forms ☐ are satisfactory. ☐ need improvement.

Trace and write.

$\mathscr{H}$ $\mathscr{H}$ ⎯ ⎯ ⎯ $\mathscr{H}$

$\mathscr{H}$ $\mathscr{H}$ ⎯ ⎯ ⎯ $\mathscr{H}$

$\mathscr{H}$ ⎯ ⎯ ⎯ ⎯ ⎯

Hi ⎯ Hu ⎯ Ho ⎯ Hy ⎯

Henri ⎯ ⎯

Harry works at
Mercy Hospital.

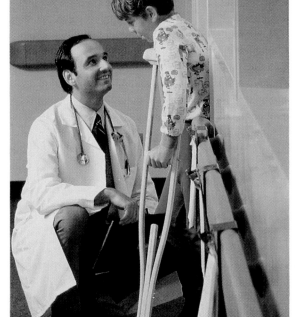

$\mathscr{H}$ ⎯ ⎯ ⎯

Trace and write.

$\mathscr{K}$ $\mathscr{K}$ $\mathscr{K}$

$\mathscr{K}$ $\mathscr{K}$ $\mathscr{K}$

$\mathscr{K}$

$\mathscr{K}e$ $\mathscr{K}a$ $\mathscr{K}y$

Krista

Kenneth

Karen is sleeping.

Kara

$\mathscr{K}$

117

Trace and write.

$\mathcal{X}$

$\mathcal{X}$ is the 24th letter of the alphabet.

$\mathcal{X}$

Explain how a xylophone is played.

Checkpoint
My letter forms are smooth. ☐ Yes ☐ No

Let's Review
H K X

This is a book for people who like cats. The book tells how small kittens grow into large cats.

How Kittens Grow

Knights of the King

Making Music with a Xylophone

How Hippo!

Write the title of the book you would read that tells about a princess who wanted to be a knight.

_____

- - - - - - - - - - - - - - - - -

_____

Write the title of the book you would read to learn how to play a musical instrument.

_____

- - - - - - - - - - - - - - - - -

_____

Write the title of the book you would read that tells about a hippopotamus.

_____

- - - - - - - - - - - - - - - - -

_____

Keys to Legibility Score Box		
Check:	Satisfactory	Needs to Improve
size	☐	☐
shape	☐	☐
slant	☐	☐
spacing	☐	☐
smoothness	☐	☐

Trace and write.

$\mathcal{V}$ $\mathcal{V}$ _____ _____ _____ $\mathcal{V}$

$\mathcal{U}$ $\mathcal{U}$ _____ _____ _____ $\mathcal{U}$

$\mathcal{U}$ _____ _____ _____ _____

$\mathcal{U}r$ _____ $\mathcal{U}n$ _____ $\mathcal{U}s$ _____

Utah has many

mountains.

$\mathcal{U}$ _____ _____ _____

Trace and write.

$\mathscr{Y}$ $\mathscr{Y}$ $\mathscr{Y}$ ———— ———— ———— $\mathscr{Y}$

$\mathscr{Y}$ $\mathscr{Y}$ $\mathscr{Y}$ ———— ———— ———— $\mathscr{Y}$

$\mathscr{Y}$ ————————————————————————

$\mathscr{Y}$ ———————————————————— $\mathscr{Y}$

$\mathscr{Y}e$ ———— $\mathscr{Y}a$ ———— $\mathscr{Y}o$ ————

$\mathscr{Y}ellowstone$ ————————————

$\mathscr{Y}osemite$ ——————————

$\mathscr{Y}ukon$ ——————

$\mathscr{Y}$ ———— ———— ————

Write about a camping trip.

121

$\mathscr{V}$

$\mathscr{V}$

$\mathscr{V}$

$\mathscr{V}$

Vera   *Van*

Victor and Vanessa

sailed from Virginia.

$\mathscr{V}$

122

Trace and write.

$\mathcal{Q}$ $\mathcal{Q}$ $\mathcal{Q}$ $\mathcal{Q}$

$\mathcal{Q}$ $\mathcal{Q}$ $\mathcal{Q}$ $\mathcal{Q}$

$\mathcal{Q}$

$\mathcal{Q}$ $\mathcal{Q}$

Quebec

Queen Elizabeth

Queen Mary

$\mathcal{Q}$

Trace and write.

Z Z Z

Z Z Z

Z

Z Z

Zi Za Zo

Zeke went to the

Detroit Zoo.

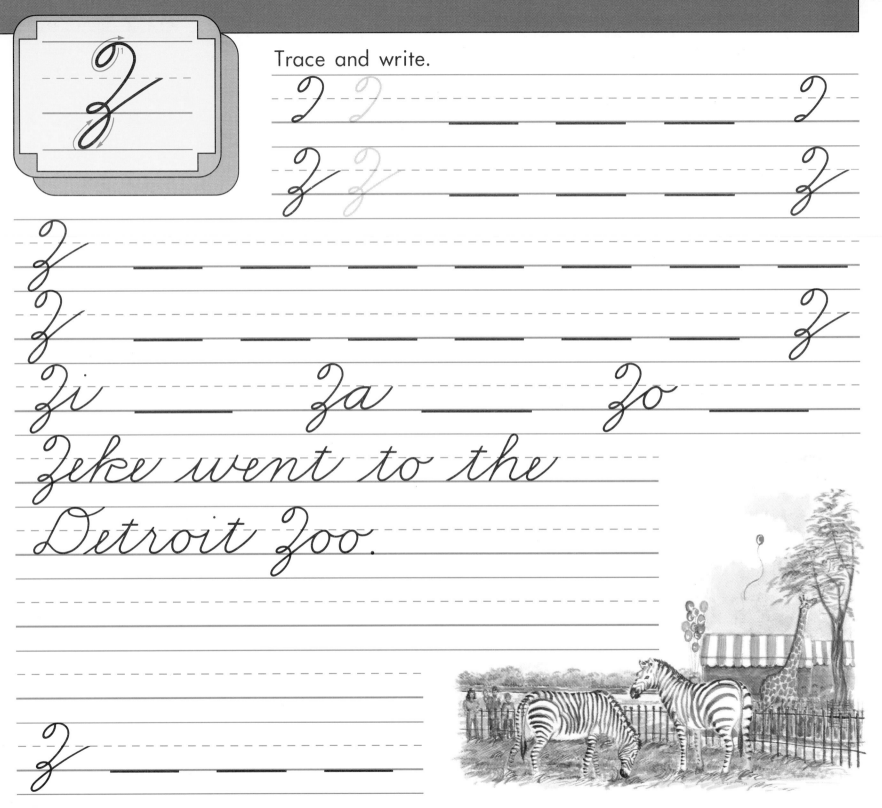

Z

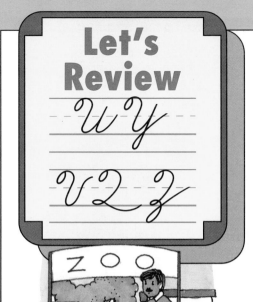

Let's Review

U Y

V Z Z

Scrambled Sentences

Write these sentences correctly.

1. *went to we Yesterday zoo. the*

2. *stripes. Zebras have*

3. *the tigers. Uncle Quincy likes*

4. *animals. treat Veterinarians*

1. _____

2. _____

3. _____

4. _____

Checkpoint The shape of my letters
☐ is satisfactory. ☐ needs to improve.

Draw a line from each person's name to the name of the job he or she does.

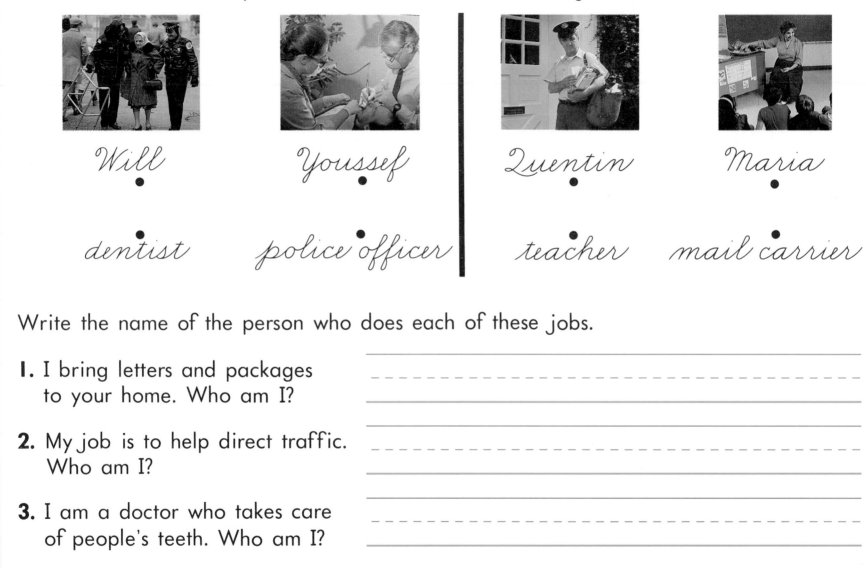

Will
•

Youssef
•

Quentin
•

Maria
•

•
dentist

•
police officer

•
teacher

•
mail carrier

Write the name of the person who does each of these jobs.

1. I bring letters and packages to your home. Who am I?

_____

2. My job is to help direct traffic. Who am I?

_____

3. I am a doctor who takes care of people's teeth. Who am I?

_____

4. I can help students learn in school. Who am I?

_____

Draw a line from each person's name to the name of the job he or she does.

Quincy •   *Zane* •   *Valerie* •   *Katie* •

mechanic •   *bus driver* •   *fire fighter* •   *doctor* •

Write the name of the person who does each of these jobs.

1. I drive students to school. Who am I?

2. I care for people when they are sick. Who am I?

3. I fix cars and trucks and make them safe to drive. Who am I?

4. My job is to put out fires and teach about fire safety. Who am I?

Forward Oval
Doublecurve Loop
Undercurve Loop

Tell Me a Story

Tell me a story
   Of castles and kings,
Of wizards and princesses,
   Magical things.

And when it is over
   And I am in bed,
The story keeps going
   Inside of my head.

Alice Low

$\mathcal{P}$

$\mathcal{P}$

$\mathcal{P}$

$\mathcal{P}$

Peter Pan

Pinocchio

Princess and the Pea

$\mathcal{P}$

Trace and write.

$\mathcal{R}$ $\mathcal{R}$ $\mathcal{R}$

$\mathcal{R}$ $\mathcal{R}$ $\mathcal{R}$

$\mathcal{R}$

Ri   Ro   Ry

Peter Rabbit

Rumpelstiltskin

Raggedy Ann

$\mathcal{R}$

131

Trace and write.

$\mathcal{B}$ $\mathcal{B}$ $\mathcal{B}$

$\mathcal{B}$ $\mathcal{B}$ $\mathcal{B}$

$\mathcal{B}$

Bert   Betty

Benji   Byron

Bambi

Black Beauty

$\mathcal{B}$

Let's Review

PRB

Winnie-the-Pooh

Edward Bear lives in the forest. His friends call him Winnie-the-Pooh. There are many funny tales about Pooh Bear and his friends, Christopher Robin, Rabbit, Piglet, Kanga, Baby Roo, Tigger, Owl, and Eeyore.

Write the names of these characters.

Pooh Bear

Christopher Robin

Rabbit _____

Piglet _____

Roo _____

Checkpoint
My letter size ☐ **is satisfactory.**
☐ **needs to improve.**

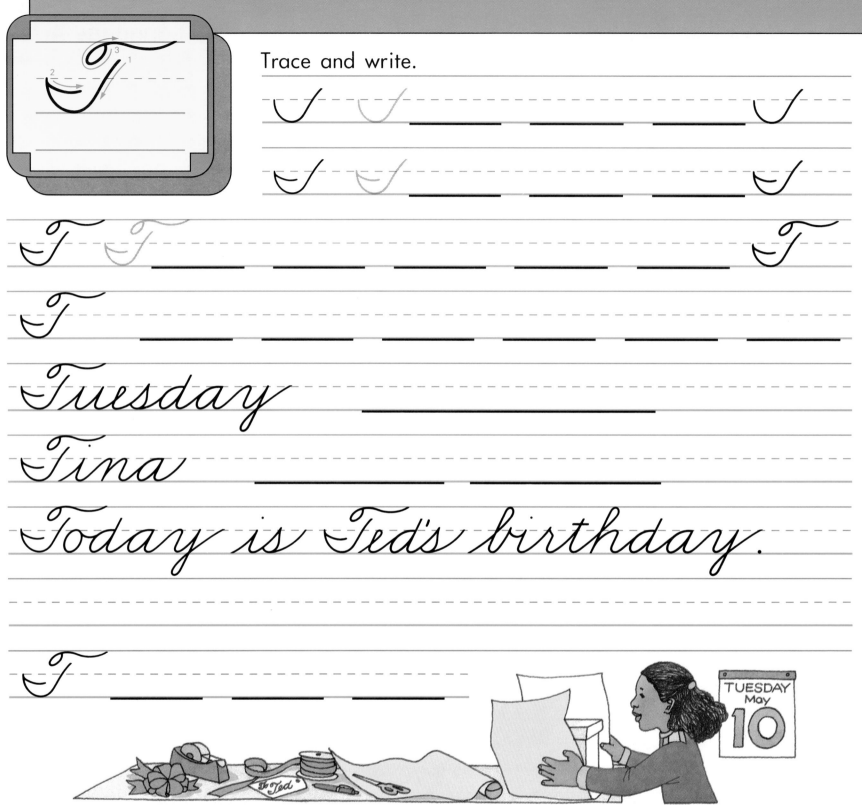

Trace and write.

Tuesday

Tina

Today is Ted's birthday.

Trace and write.

$\mathcal{F}$ $\mathcal{F}$ _____ _____ _____ $\mathcal{F}$

$\mathcal{F}$ $\mathcal{F}$ _____ _____ _____ $\mathcal{F}$

$\mathcal{F}$ _____ _____ _____ _____ _____

$\mathcal{F}$ _____ _____ _____ _____ _____ $\mathcal{F}$

February _____

Fran's birthday is

in February.

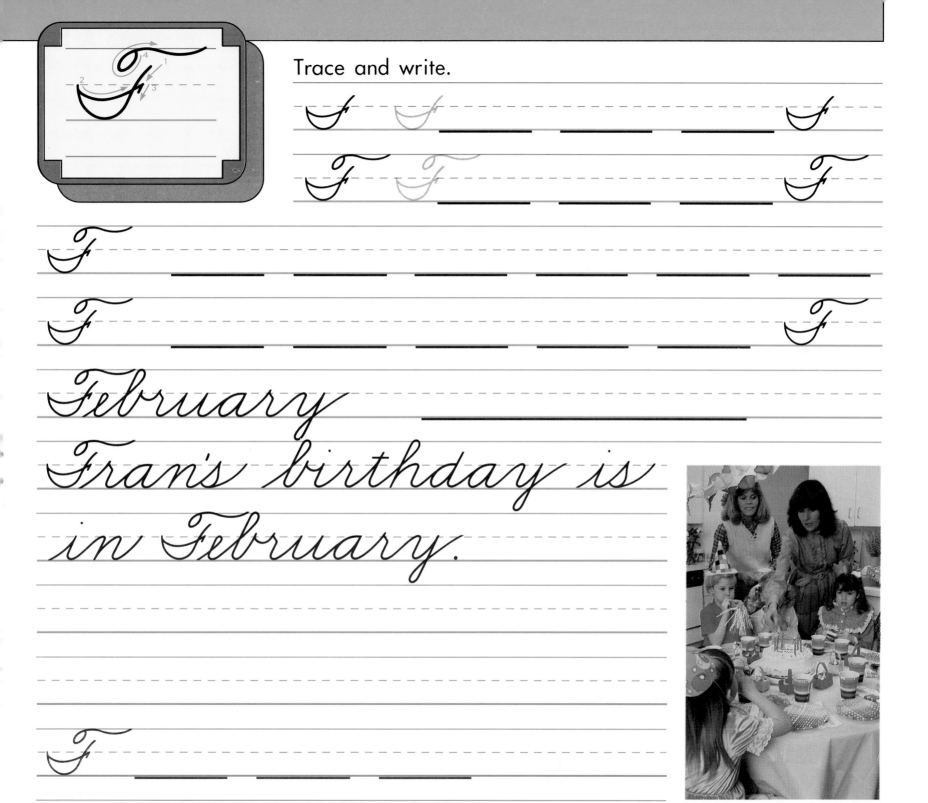

$\mathcal{F}$ _____ _____ _____

Let's Review

Ff

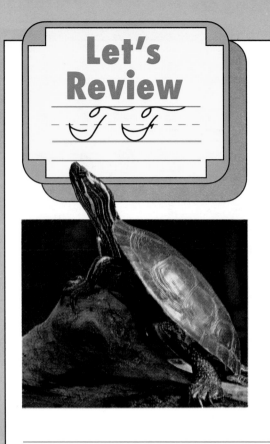

Write the title and the first two lines of the poem.

Thomas F. Turtle

Thomas F. Turtle has
such a strange house.
He hasn't a key to the door;
He hasn't a window; he hasn't
a porch;
And the roof is a lot like the floor.
Kathryn Gelander

Keys to Legibility Score Box		
Check:	**Satisfactory**	**Needs to Improve**
size	☐	☐
shape	☐	☐
slant	☐	☐
spacing	☐	☐
smoothness	☐	☐

Trace and write.

g g g

g g g

G G G

G

Greg   Gloria

Grandfather Gates works

in his garden.

G

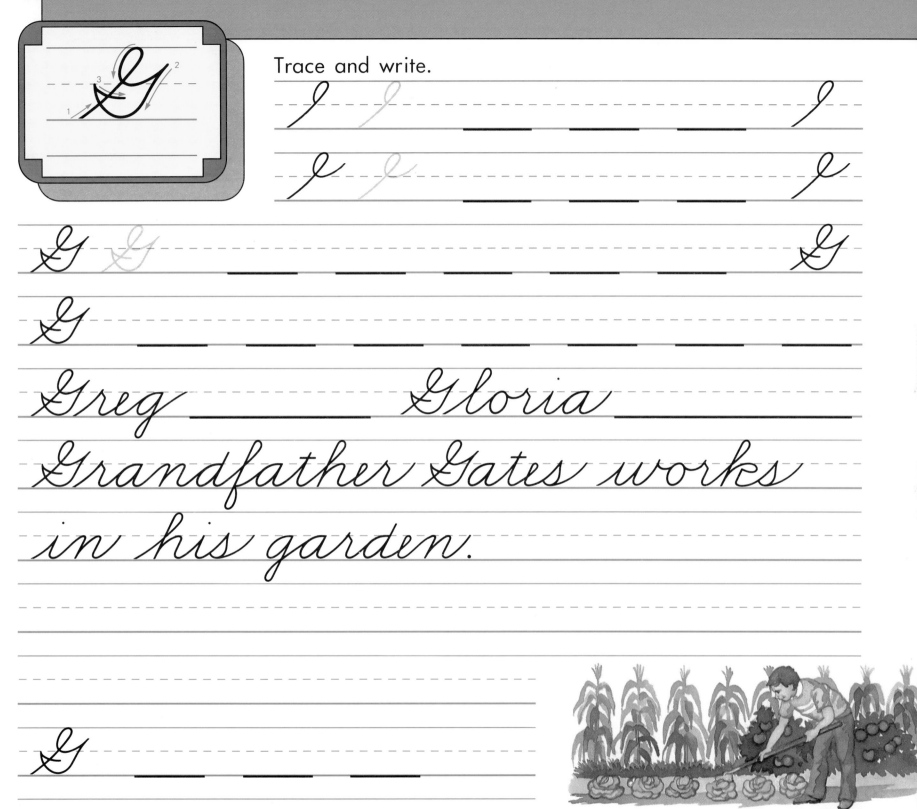

137

Trace and write.

$\mathcal{S}$

$\mathcal{S}$

$\mathcal{S}$

$\mathcal{S}$

September

Spinach is Susan's

favorite vegetable.

$\mathcal{S}$

Trace and write.

$\mathcal{L}$ $\mathcal{L}$ _____ _____ _____ $\mathcal{L}$

$\mathcal{J}$ $\mathcal{J}$ _____ _____ _____ $\mathcal{J}$

$\mathcal{L}$ $\mathcal{L}$ _____ _____ _____ $\mathcal{L}$

$\mathcal{L}$ _____ _____ _____ _____

Leo _____ Leanne _____

Listen carefully to

Lisa's directions.

$\mathcal{L}$ _____ _____ _____

Some animals make their homes on land.
Other animals live in the sea.

Write the categories *Land* and *Sea*.
Write the names of the six animals that belong
in each category.

Starfish	Lobster
Squirrel	Rabbit
Leopard	Perch
Fox	Sea Turtle
Giraffe	Shark
Guppy	Bear

1. _____
2. _____
3. _____
4. _____
5. _____
6. _____

1. _____
2. _____
3. _____
4. _____
5. _____
6. _____

Keys to Legibility Score Box

Check:	Satisfactory	Needs to Improve
size	☐	☐
shape	☐	☐
slant	☐	☐
spacing	☐	☐
smoothness	☐	☐

Posttest

Write the first verse. Use your best handwriting.

Look in a Book

Look in a book
and you will see
words and magic
and mystery.

Look in a book
and you will find
sense and nonsense
of every kind.

Look in a book
and you will know
all the things that
can help you grow.

Ivy O. Eastwick

Keys to Legibility Score Box		
Check:	Satisfactory	Needs to Improve
size	☐	☐
shape	☐	☐
slant	☐	☐
spacing	☐	☐
smoothness	☐	☐

Student Record of Handwriting Skills

Manuscript/Cursive

	Needs Improvement	Mastery of Skill
Writes manuscript basic strokes.	☐	☐
Positions paper properly for manuscript writing.	☐	☐
Holds pencil properly.	☐	☐
Writes manuscript **I, L, i, I, t, T.**	☐	☐
Writes manuscript numerals.	☐	☐
Writes manuscript **o, O, a, A, d, D, c, C, e, E, f, F.**	☐	☐
Writes manuscript **g, G, j, J, q, Q, u, U, s, S, b, B.**	☐	☐
Writes manuscript **p, P, r, R, n, N, m, M, h, H.**	☐	☐
Writes punctuation marks.	☐	☐
Writes manuscript **v, V, y, Y, w, W, k, K, x, X, z, Z.**	☐	☐
Positions paper properly for cursive writing.	☐	☐
Writes cursive basic strokes.	☐	☐
Writes cursive **i, t, u, w, e.**	☐	☐
Writes cursive **l, b, h, k.**	☐	☐

	Needs Improvement	Mastery of Skill
Writes cursive **r, s, f, p, j.**	☐	☐
Writes cursive **a, d, g, q, o, c.**	☐	☐
Writes cursive **n, m, v, x, y, z.**	☐	☐
Writes cursive numerals.	☐	☐
Writes cursive **A, O, D, C, E.**	☐	☐
Writes cursive **I, J.**	☐	☐
Writes cursive **N, M, W.**	☐	☐
Writes cursive **H, K, X.**	☐	☐
Writes cursive **U, Y, V, Q, Z.**	☐	☐
Writes cursive **P, R, B.**	☐	☐
Writes cursive **T, F.**	☐	☐
Writes cursive **G, S, L.**	☐	☐
Writes slant correctly.	☐	☐
Writes smoothness correctly.	☐	☐
Writes shape correctly.	☐	☐
Writes size correctly.	☐	☐
Writes spacing correctly.	☐	☐

Good Sitting Position

- Sit comfortably.
- Place both arms on the table with the elbows just off the desk.
- Keep feet flat on the floor.

How to Hold Your Pencil

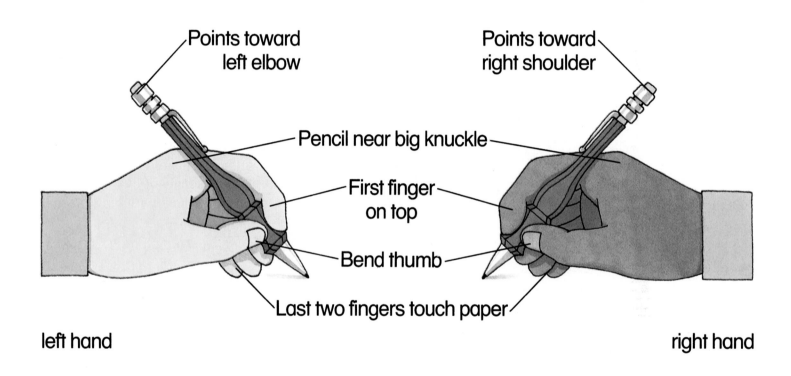

Points toward
left elbow

Points toward
right shoulder

Pencil near big knuckle

First finger
on top

Bend thumb

Last two fingers touch paper

left hand

right hand

Paper Position for Manuscript Writing

left hand

right hand

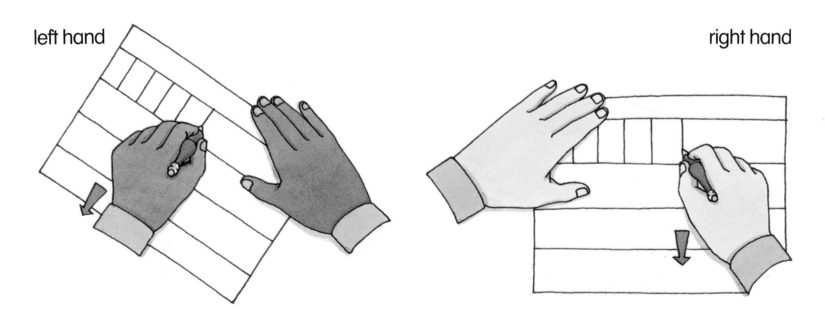

Pull
downstrokes
toward the
left elbow.

Pull
downstrokes
toward the
midsection.

Paper Position for Cursive Writing

left hand

right hand

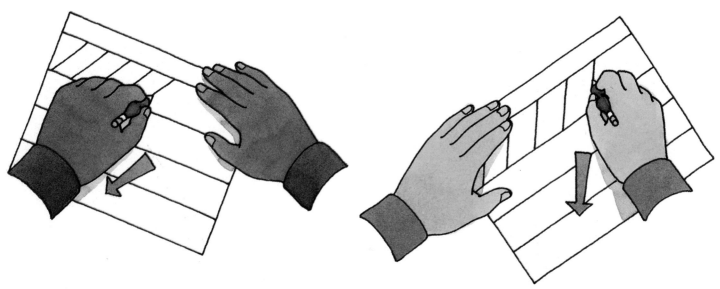

Pull
downstrokes
toward the
left elbow.

Pull
downstrokes
toward the
midsection.